ROY CASTLE REMEMBERED

ROY CASTLE REMEMBERED

Fellow stars, friends, fans and family recall the great entertainer

compiled by

Ray Donnelly FRCSE

CHIVERS LARGE PRINT
BATH

British Library Cataloguing in Publication Data available

This Large Print edition published by Chivers Press, Bath, 1996.

Published by arrangement with Robson Books Limited

U.K. Hardcover ISBN 0 7451 4928 6
U.K. Softcover   ISBN 0 7451 4929 4

Photoset, printed and bound in Great Britain by
Redwood Books, Trowbridge, Wiltshire

To all Roy's friends and fans whose memories of a most lovable and exceptional man made this book possible.

ACKNOWLEDGEMENTS

I would like to express my appreciation of the great skills and commitment of Louise Dixon who has contributed so much to the preparation of this book and to Dorothy Foulds, who has given freely many hours of dedicated secretarial help.

CONTENTS

INTRODUCTION

by Ray Donnelly FRCSE

'Yes, you can use my name, but I won't be able to do much for you because I'm not very well.' This was Roy's answer when we asked him to give his name to a special Appeal for the Lung Cancer Fund to build an International Centre for Lung Cancer Research. In the months that followed, the whole nation saw what Roy *could* do and witnessed the most remarkable example of courage, commitment, integrity and faith imbued throughout with great good humour in the most difficult of circumstances.

It was at Roy's Memorial Service in London that the idea of this book came to me. People there had so many happy and funny stories to tell about him that I felt they should be collected together and written down so that they would not be lost. I then set about soliciting anecdotes and memories from Roy's colleagues and friends and from his fans all over the country.

The response was overwhelming and the task of deciding which to leave out proved to be extremely difficult. Those which appear in the book have been abbreviated and edited to suit the format and I hope the contributors will excuse me for doing this. To those who have been left out, I can only say thank you for giving me your own insight into this wonderful man and perhaps we will be able to include them in another edition.

I have so many of my own memories of Roy, although I only met him for the first time in 1992. I had established the Lung Cancer Fund as a new charity the year before and he came to Liverpool to launch a street poster campaign for the Fund. On that occasion, I took him to visit the Cardiothoracic Centre, where I work, to meet some other lung cancer patients.

Although not well himself at the time, he visited all the wards and I was enormously impressed by the way in which he was able to relate personally to each one he met and to make them laugh with different stories and jokes. He had a troublesome cough and looked as if he had a temperature but he did not spare himself and I had my first glimpse of the self giving which would be demonstrated a hundredfold in the remaining months of his life.

Roy had a marvellous ability to make people feel happy and my abiding memory of him will be that great big smile which was so genuine and attractive and could light up an arena the size of Anfield football ground.

The effect of Roy's involvement on our fundraising was phenomenal and the charity rapidly acquired a national identity, although most people knew it as the Roy Castle Cause for Hope Appeal. In recognition of the huge impact made by Roy on the development of the charity, the Trustees agreed to change its name from the Lung Cancer Fund to the Roy Castle Cause for Hope Foundation and it was entirely appropriate that this should be done.

Since Roy died, the momentum has been maintained and this is due to the continued dedication of Fiona, who has picked up and run with the torch lit by Roy, and the phenomenal commitment and ability of Sylvia Ingham, her team and all our supporters.

The Foundation is now firmly established on the national scene and has formed strong international links. It will stimulate and finance lung cancer research throughout the United Kingdom and will develop vigorous preventative programmes, particularly among the young. It will, in due course, make a significant contribution to the eventual elimination of this dreadful disease and future generations will have much cause to be thankful for the life of the man who is happily remembered by his friends and fans in this book.

Ray Donnelly FRCSE
Founder and Chairman of Trustees,
The Roy Castle Cause for Hope Foundation

FOREWORD
by Fiona Castle

I must be the most privileged person I know! Imagine having the opportunity to write the Foreword for a book filled with other people's memories of the man to whom you were married for thirty-one years? What a treat for the possible future generations of the Castle line.

When it comes to my memories, it's difficult to express just a few. Roy is still so much a part of my life that it will take a long time for him to become simply a memory. That's why it's so heartening to read so many affectionate reminiscences in this book.

Since Roy's death, the admiration and warmth of those who loved him have continued to pour in—not only in the form of letters from the many fans he held so dear, but also in the continuing response to the Cause for Hope. Roy was very committed to the project and when I expressed concern that the momentum he had built up might be lost after his death, he simply said, 'You wait. It will *gather* momentum'—and he was right. The wave of love he experienced on the Train of Hope and at the various sell-out concerts held around Britain continues even now.

Ray Donnelly—whose brainchild this book is—is the most extraordinary man. His quiet, gentle character belies the steely determination with which he brings ideas to fruition, sweeping people along and bearing them up with his enthusiasm. It was this charisma which inspired Roy to become involved with the Cause of Hope Foundation in the first place. He little realized then that it would consume his final days with his own passion to see a lung cancer research centre built and operating, employing top of the range specialists to find a cure for the disease which finally called an end to his life on earth.

I am so grateful to all those who have contributed—many great friends and show business colleagues as well as those unknown to Roy save for a chance meeting in a shop or at a function. I am warmed by the generous and humorous nature of these observations, aware that although Roy was a very ordinary, down-to-earth human being, he had a gift for seeing the funny side of life and an affection for people which never waned.

Thank you, Ray, for the painstaking hours you have spent compiling and writing such a record—more evidence of your ingenuity and skill for fundraising.

Thank you to all who have contributed to the book—and to all you who have contributed to the fundraising by buying the book.

'My cup of joy runneth over'
(Psalm 23)

I

CAUSE FOR HOPE

SYLVIA INGHAM

Chief Executive, Roy Castle Cause for Hope Foundation

The first time I met Roy was on a cold December morning in 1993. I had arrived at his home with a film crew from Border TV to film a promotional video about the Lung Cancer Fund. Fiona met us at the door with a happy smile, but informed us that Roy was not feeling at all well and that he was resting until we had everything set up ready for filming. Fiona made us so welcome and said that Roy was expecting a call from his specialist as he had been coughing and feeling unwell for some weeks.

We settled in and set up for the filming and then Roy came into the room. You would have thought that there was absolutely nothing wrong with him, his big smile and bubbly personality totally amazed us all.

Half-way through the filming Roy's specialist called and confirmed the sad news that Roy's tumour had returned and that his battle against lung cancer was on again. Roy remained so cheerful—I could not believe the courage of this wonderful man. On my return to the Lung Cancer Fund's base in Liverpool, I faxed Roy to thank him for giving us his time

3 ⬧

on such an awful day, and also told him about Ray Donnelly's idea to launch an appeal to build the world's first Lung Cancer Research Centre and that Ray wanted Roy to put his name to the appeal. The fax had only just gone through and Roy phoned me.

'Let's go for it!' he said. 'We have to do something to stop the number of people dying from lung cancer. I want our children and our grandchildren not to have to go through what *our* families are experiencing.'

He then said, 'You know I'm ill and I can give you my name but I won't be able to do very much else.'

Well, we have all seen what Roy did! So was born the Roy Castle Cause for Hope Appeal.

COLIN & PAMELA LAWRENCE

Our most treasured memory of Roy is when our daughter, Nicola, was invited to spend a day with him and Fiona at their home in Gerrards Cross.

Nicola, who was only twenty-five years old, had just been diagnosed as having lung cancer. She was devastated. Soon after her diagnosis, she was getting ready to go out with friends when she heard Roy on the television programme *Going Live*. He was chatting about a little boy who said to him, 'You can't die 'cos you're my hero.' Roy went on to say how those words had encouraged him to carry on fighting and he chatted about his illness, the future and how he felt. This too was how Nicola felt and he in turn gave her encouragement. She became determined to fight like Roy. About two weeks later, after people from the Lung Cancer Fund had contacted Roy, he wrote to Nicola inviting her to visit him. Nicola was flown to his home where she was made to feel very welcome. Fiona even baked her a 'Welcome Nicola' cake. Roy and Nicola spent the day discussing the illness and the future. There was lots of laughing and joking and he even played his trumpet for her. She was so taken with him and remarked to him, 'If you can do that after all the treatment it must be working and there's a chance for me.'

During the day Nicola told Roy all about her own 'Appeal' which eventually raised over £100,000 for the Lung Cancer Fund. Roy was very touched and impressed. He immediately pledged to help her and went on to give his full support to the Lung Cancer Fund through the Roy Castle Cause for Hope Appeal.

Nicola was very poorly that day but she didn't complain as she didn't want to spoil a wonderfully happy day with Roy. He made her much more relaxed and at ease with things. On the way back to Liverpool Nicola's plane had to touch down in Birmingham because she was so unwell but, on her return, she told us about her visit and what a marvellous, kind, caring and sincere person Roy was. Unfortunately, this was the last day Nicola ever went out. She was too ill and days later was taken to hospital where she died on 16 February 1993.

As soon as he heard of Nicola's death, Roy phoned us at home to say how sorry he was and that he would carry on raising money for the Fund which he did for as long as he possibly could.

We thank Roy for giving her such a marvellous day when she was feeling so low.

ROGER PHILLIPS

In January 1994, I was privileged to compère the Liverpool launch of the Roy Castle Cause for Hope Appeal in the magnificent setting of St George's Hall. I was on stage, therefore, when Roy made his appearance.

He had the most extraordinary effect on the audience—not because of the Appeal, not because of his jokes or his trumpet playing. The secret lay in his smile. He just radiated a feeling of happiness which contacted and communicated with everyone in the hall. From my vantage point, you could see that smile transmit to every person there. It was simply glorious.

ARTHUR JOHNSON

I first met Roy on Sunday 13 March 1994. It was to be the start of a close, but brief, friendship. A few weeks after the meeting the *Liverpool Echo* officially adopted the Appeal and I was seconded to work on the project.

It was a historic day on Merseyside—the last derby match before the standing Kop was demolished to be replaced by an all-seater stand. Liverpool FC had agreed that a collection for the Appeal could be made at the ground and I had helped arrange for Roy to lead the teams out in front of the capacity crowd.

My wife and I travelled to the ground with Roy, Fiona and Sylvia Ingham, the chief executive of the Appeal. It was a cold, early spring Sunday and Fiona made sure Roy was wrapped up warm, with his bobble hat firmly on his bald head.

We spent an hour or so touring the executive boxes at the ground, receiving corporate donations to the Appeal. Then Brian Hall, the club's public relations director, said Roy was needed on the other side of the ground for a television interview. The stadium had started to fill and the only way of getting to the interview was for us to walk in front of the Kop, now more than half full.

Because Roy wanted the full impact of his appearance to come when he led the teams out, he turned his collar up, pulled his hat down over his ears, tucked his chin deep into his chest and we started to walk in single file across the pitch, only a yard or so in front of the great bank of fans standing and singing on the Kop.

We were just half-way across when I heard a single fan call 'Look it's him, Roy Castle!' Roy knew the game was up. He turned and looked over his shoulder at me. I could tell from the twinkle in his eyes he was going to go for it—and he did!

He pulled the hat from his head, held his arms aloft and the greatest football choir in the world started to roar: 'There's only one Roy Castle, There's only one Roy Castle ...'

As long as I live I shall never forget standing there, part of this small group, as huge waves of sound and love rolled over us. The emotion was so strong you could touch it.

But this was more than just about emotion. This was a very wise choir and they had it right that day—there was only one Roy Castle.

BRIAN HALL

I only ever met Roy Castle once, but it was an occasion I will never forget.

In March 1994 at the Liverpool v Everton match at Anfield, the Cause for Hope Appeal held a collection which raised a staggering £10,000. Roy honoured the club with his presence, visiting the private boxes and hospitality suites. Everywhere he went he had a smile, a chat and an autograph for everyone, even though he was obviously a very sick man.

When Roy led out the teams prior to kick off, he received an incredible welcome from Liverpool and Everton supporters alike. A chant echoed around the whole stadium, with 45,000 people singing 'There's only one Roy Castle'.

ROBERT POWELL

My favourite memory of Roy is in fact one of the last memories I have of him. In June 1994 we travelled up to Liverpool together to launch a lottery in aid of the Cause for Hope Appeal. During the trip Roy told me that it was only through luck that he had been able to make the trip at all, as the drugs he was taking meant that some days he was completely incapacitated. This day, however, was a good day.

After the launch, during which Roy had made it hard to believe he was even ill, we were invited to have lunch at Littlewoods' Head Office. It was a small private lunch that I will never forget. A casual remark about working in Variety theatres was all that was needed. For the next fifteen minutes Roy regaled the guests with stories. I remember looking round the table at faces crying, not with compassion but with laughter.

Roy was an extraordinary man with an extraordinary ability and I'd seen him perform many times but I'll never forget the laughter of that day in Liverpool. To me it summed him up, a man who even in the last months of his life conducted himself without a trace of self pity and all the humility and generosity that we'd become used to over the years.

I was proud to know him.

JOHN MOORES

I first met Roy Castle at a lunch at Littlewoods' Head Office in Liverpool, after Littlewoods had agreed to sponsor the Tour of Hope, a three-day 1,200-mile tour of Great Britain which Roy undertook despite medical advice. The lunch was a happy occasion as Roy encouraged everyone to get involved and think of ideas for fundraising, as well as entertaining us all with his memories of Liverpool and appearances at the Empire Theatre.

On being asked how he discovered he had lung cancer, Roy described waking one night with a very severe headache and feeling desperately ill. He was taken into hospital for tests. They could not find out exactly what was wrong, but his blood tests had thrown up some unusual results.

The doctors asked Roy to restrict his intake of liquids for a few days, after which he felt a little better. He was allowed gradually to increase his liquid intake and immediately felt unwell again. Further tests were done.

Eventually the results of the tests came through and he was told, 'You've got twice as much water in your blood as you should have.'

'Cor!' he said, 'that would have killed Oliver Reed!' He could see humour in every situation—no matter how serious.

SIR CLIFF RICHARD

My abiding memory is of Roy on stage at the Liverpool Empire, beaming and blinking into the spotlight and accepting the standing ovation of a cheering capacity audience. A moment before he had moved them to tears and to laughter with a speech which required every ounce of courage, determination and professionalism.

Neither Roy, Fiona, nor any of us knew whether he was going to make it on stage for the finale of the Cause for Hope Appeal concert in the summer of 1994. It was what he called one of his 'bad' days, and in the dressing-room he looked drained of every human resource. He could barely summon the energy to stand, and his cough was particularly troublesome. He had been travelling the country, promoting the Appeal, talking to the media, and agreeing to countless photo calls. It had taken its toll, and now he'd arrived for the focal event, utterly exhausted.

Roy was due to follow me on stage after my few songs, but I was expecting an 'ad lib' finale without him. I should have known better. After the first two or three shaky steps on the arm of Gerry Marsden, Roy walked unaided into the spotlight, seemed to grow a full six inches in stature, and captivated everyone with the bravest performance that any artist can ever have given.

Whether it was God's Spirit, adrenalin, or showbiz instinct, I don't know—I suspect it was a mix of all three—but suddenly, for five wonderful minutes, Roy was transformed. It was as if he put aside his vulnerability to smile, to stand tall, and to be an inspiration.

I, along with the thousands who were privileged to be at the Liverpool Empire on that day, will remember him with immense gratitude.

SIR JOHN MILLS

There have been many occasions during my life that I shall never forget. The following is one of them. In fact, it has to be top of the list.

One evening in July 1994, I was waiting in the wings of the Empire Theatre in Liverpool. Sitting beside me was Roy Castle and his wife, Fiona. The occasion was to raise money for the Cause for Hope Appeal and this amazing man had started at 8.30 am on the platform of Euston Station in London. I arrived at 11 am to find him touring around on a luggage cart giving radio and television interviews. He then boarded the train where he gave more interviews. He was seriously ill and was kept going by injections, but no one would ever have known it.

In the evening he waited for 2½ hours before his appearance at the theatre and a few minutes before he was due to go on stage I couldn't believe that he would make it. He was very weak and could hardly stand. Then a miracle happened.

He was announced, he stood up straight as a ramrod and walked firmly on to the stage where he was received with the biggest ovation I have ever heard in any theatre in the world. He proceeded to make a marvellous speech, full of laughs. The only thing, he said, was that it would not be possible for him to blow his trumpet. I have never seen such an act of courage in my life. It was the last time that Roy was to appear on stage anywhere and I shall always feel it has been a privilege and an honour to be part of that unforgettable evening.

PHILIP LOVE

I have two great regrets about Roy Castle. The first, his death and the second, the fact that I never met him. My knowledge of him was limited to what I read about him—a great deal—and to what I saw of him on television—a lively, cheery and highly accomplished entertainer. I shall never forget his great courage and dignity. This was particularly in evidence when he and his wife, Fiona, took part in a very special BBC *Songs of Praise* programme which was a most moving and memorable broadcast. Roy's fortitude in the face of the greatest adversity of all was a marvellous tribute to the power of faith and trust in God.

Roy was much loved by so many people and held in such high regard that, unprompted, five members of the security staff of the University of Liverpool, of which I am Vice-Chancellor, volunteered to embark upon a marathon 'Walk of Hope' in aid of the Cause for Hope Appeal. They received support from many other members of staff at the University and from twenty-two other universities throughout the UK. That marathon, from Edinburgh to London, raised over £30,000 for the Appeal. Such was the effect Roy Castle had on the ordinary man and woman in the street who had never met him!

Like so many of the staff at the University, I feel that I have lost a very good friend. Roy Castle will never be forgotten and the Lung Cancer Research Centre in Liverpool will be a fitting memorial to a quite remarkable man.

THE MOST REV. DEREK WORLOCK

Archbishop of Liverpool

It was shortly after it became known in 1992 that Roy Castle had been diagnosed as suffering from lung cancer that, quite suddenly, the same thing happened to me. I was more fortunate than he, in that it was judged that my troubles were operable. So whilst I suffered the removal of one lung, before enduring four months of chemotherapy, I read various accounts of Roy's steady improvement in health and his courage in sharing his problems with the general public.

I had also decided that my own trials should be fully public at the time of the operation, so that people might be encouraged by the fact that we were not ashamed of the disease with which we had been afflicted.

As I grew stronger I became Patron and then Vice-President of the Lung Cancer Fund, now renamed the Roy Castle Cause for Hope Foundation. Through my surgeon, Ray Donnelly, Chairman of the Fund, I came to know more about Roy's ups and downs, even though they were nearly always reported in the press as progress.

It was in the autumn of 1993 that I learned

20

of the recurrence of Roy's lung cancer. His courage in facing still more chemotherapy was remarkable and must surely have put even his good spirits to the test. I was surprised to learn that he felt able to take part that Christmas in the production of *Pickwick*, with his old friend Sir Harry Secombe, at the Alexandra Theatre, Birmingham.

It so happened that I was staying with friends at the New Year and we decided to take advantage of some tickets they had been given and went to the theatre on New Year's night.

The theatre was filled to bursting point and it was a splendid performance, with Roy, complete in wig, playing the part of Sam Weller's father. With a radio-mike he managed splendidly and the whole audience, as well as the cast, were willing him on.

At the end of the performance, Sir Harry came forward and suggested we should all sing 'Auld Lang Syne' and we rose, joined arms, and did so. Roy and Harry, centre-stage, led the singing and then proceeded to cavort around the stage whilst the audience cheered them on. I shall never forget the sheer exuberance of Roy as he moved towards the back-drop, turned and waved his wig at the audience and disappeared out of sight.

I was very moved by this and the following day wrote to him to congratulate him. I told him that I knew how flat he must be feeling that morning, what it had cost him to entertain in such generous fashion and how we all wished him well. I had a postcard back almost by return, with a message from 'Sir H' and lots of thanks and good wishes.

It was at this stage that Roy came to Liverpool to launch the Roy Castle Cause for Hope Appeal. We appeared together on the same platform and both realized how personally we were concerned with the outcome of the Appeal.

The rest of Roy's story is well known. It is not always appreciated that he became a baptized Christian that Easter and drew deeply on his faith and that of Fiona, in the months which followed. We exchanged a number of letters and messages and his bravery, as he grew weaker, was an astonishing witness in a society better known for its secularist standards. We were in touch until the end, and then afterwards Fiona told me of his devotion to the Gethsemane prayer of Christ, which in Roy's words became, 'Lord, I don't want to die, but if that's the way you want it, it's OK with me.'

Such faith and courage have already proved to be a great inspiration to those carrying on the work for the Cause for Hope Foundation. The extent to which we can all follow this through will greatly affect the number of those who will benefit from the research inspired by his memory.

LINDA McDERMOTT

I've interviewed cabinet ministers and film stars without batting an eyelid, but on the morning that Roy Castle was due on my radio programme, I was tense.

I spoke to our reception staff at BBC Radio Merseyside and told them to make sure that Roy was made comfortable as soon as he entered the building. I asked my producer to make sure that he was given a seat as soon as he arrived in the studio, and offered a cup of tea or coffee. I also told her that the interview would probably be very short as I didn't wish to put too much strain on a man who was already critically ill.

Roy entered the studio just after the news. Not that the word 'entered' adequately describes his arrival. He breezed into the studio with a big smile on his face, and when he had checked that the microphones were not live, he came over and gave me a big hug. For the next half hour he kept me and my listeners entranced with his bubbly personality, telling us stories of his life and career. At one point he even broke into song.

When he had gone, my producer and I looked at each other in amazement. Roy had been one of the liveliest guests we'd had on the programme for months, yet we had almost expected him to be pushed into the studio in a wheelchair.

Half an hour after Roy had left, several rounds of toast arrived for me and the programme team—Roy had ordered them from the café next door!

I'm sure that doing the radio interview took a great deal out of Roy and it wouldn't surprise me if he was exhausted for hours afterwards. But as I was to find out in the coming months, Roy would always put on a brave face for his audience; that was an aspect of his great courage.

JOHN GRIFFITHS

I was just a face in the crowd. Roy Castle did not know me. But of course, I knew him. After all, he had been one of Britain's best-known entertainers for many years and I had grown up with Roy, the trumpet-playing tap-dancing entertainer, through to Roy the *Record Breaker*, entertaining my own children on TV.

But the man I was waiting to cheer on at Liverpool's Lime Street station as he embarked on the nationwide Tour of Hope was not Roy Castle the entertainer, but Roy Castle the inspiration. His personal example of courage and commitment had transformed the Cause for Hope Appeal from an ambitious dream to reality, and his transparent determination to turn his own misfortune into positive achievement had made the Yorkshireman an honorary Scouser in record time.

Despite the close working relationship between Roy's appeal and the *Liverpool Echo*, of which I am editor, our paths had not crossed. And though I looked forward to meeting him one day, I wanted to be a part of the bond that had developed between Roy Castle and the so-called ordinary people of Merseyside. One of the crowd, not one of the media reporting on events and trying to remain detached from the mood.

Journalists are a privileged bunch. They get in on the inside track where the public is not allowed to go. But on that day my privilege was to be one of many, and share in the extraordinary mood as the public literally willed Roy on as he bravely embarked on a nationwide tour despite his frailty.

The band played and the mood was celebratory as a Rolls-Royce pulled up on the station platform. But the mood changed as a desperately sick man got out, watched by an anxious Ray Donnelly, the cancer surgeon who knew only too well how ill Roy Castle really was. Then an amazing thing happened. A wave of love and warmth washed across the platform, and Roy was clearly buoyed up by it.

He straightened, he smiled, he waved. He gave a brief speech and then he picked out a child in the crowd for a special message of hope for future generations. The appeal simply had to succeed. It was for the children and the future, he said.

There wasn't a dry eye on the station platform, and there wasn't a man, woman or child who did not know that this journey could well be Roy's last. It was an effort of will that will never be forgotten by anyone there on that day. And if it lifted Roy, it also inspired those working with him to re-double their efforts and make his dream come true.

You cannot measure the power of

admiration and affection. You can't even see it. But when it hits you with such force as it did that day, you certainly can feel it. As a spiritual man, Roy Castle would know that, and his family would too.

We never met in the sense of shaking hands and saying hello. But like everyone else in the crowd around me, I felt I had been lucky to cross the path of an inspirational man.

We were all VIPs that day.

JOHNNY KENNEDY

Early in 1994, I chatted with Roy Castle after the launch of his Lung Cancer Appeal at the St George's Hall in Liverpool. Despite his illness he was bouncy and cheerful and a few minutes earlier had entertained the large audience with a few jokes and a breezy version of 'When the Saints Go Marching In' on his trumpet.

I told him I was going to run in the New York Marathon in November to raise money for the Appeal, and he seemed genuinely pleased. I told him that the marathon was to be televised on Sky Sports, so he'd be able to watch it, and I still remember his reply, 'I won't be around to watch Sky Sports in November, but I'll certainly be watching you from up in the sky!'

I laughed and said I was sure he'd still be with us, but he just smiled and shook his head.

Roy's bravery that summer inspired the nation, but finally he lost the battle ... just as he knew he would.

In November I stood on the starting line on Staten Island with over 29,000 runners in the New York Marathon. For the first few miles it rained, which suited me, and when I passed the Williamsburg Bank in Brooklyn, eight miles in, I was feeling fine. This was my 56th marathon so I know a bit about them by now. I keep myself to myself and try not to get involved in conversations with other runners. I just lock myself into the race and pop along at a nice steady pace.

The New York Marathon goes through Queens, Manhattan, the South Bronx and Harlem. It gives you some spectacular views of the famous skyline and it takes you down streets where life on an ordinary day must be harsh and dangerous.

I reached the top of Fifth Avenue with about five miles to go and began to feel less than good. It's a thing that happens in marathons and you learn to accept it, though it was made a little bit more difficult on this occasion by a painful blister on my left foot. I was feeling a little bit sorry for myself—and five miles suddenly seemed rather a long way. I plodded on past 114th Street, still twelve blocks away from Central Park, knowing that even when I reached the park I still had three miles to go. At this point I was not enjoying the New York Marathon.

And then—let the cynics scoff—thoughts of Roy Castle came into my head and it was as though I could hear him urging me on. It only seemed to last for a few seconds but it made an amazing difference. My stride picked up and I forgot all about the blister.

With two miles to go, a friend from the New York Road Runners Club called out to me as I ran past, and told me later that I had looked strong and fresh.

I finished in three hours twenty-nine minutes in 3704th position out of 29,628 finishers and, as far as I'm concerned, some of the credit goes to Roy Castle.

II

EARLY DAYS

DOROTHY MEYRICK

My father, Dr Edward Trotter, of Scholes, Holmfirth, brought 'our Roy' into the world on 31 August 1932. Roy and his family lived just along the road from us.

I was twenty and nursing in London when Roy was born, but my youngest sister, Mary, was six. Mary and Roy used to fish together in the Mill Dam nearby.

My mother always took an interest in Roy, helping to pay for his tap-dancing lessons and giving him a satchel when he went to Honley Grammar School in Huddersfield.

I last saw Roy about eight years ago at our Grand Theatre here in Swansea—he had his own evening. I went to see him in his dressing-room after the show and he said to me, 'Ee Dorothy, it's good to see thee! How's your Mary? Is she still fishing?' (she is!) 'Your Dad and Mum—Dr and Mrs Trotter—were like the Mayor and Mayoress of Scholes!'

NANCY TROTTER

Roy's mother was either a hairdresser or dressmaker in Scholes and I remember being told by some member of my family that at the age of three 'our Roy' used to be put up on a table to dance to entertain the customers while they were waiting—so obviously his talents were inborn! When he was a bit older he was the star turn at the Old Folk's Treat held in my sister's garden at Brockholes.

EDWARD TURNER

I was born in the next village to Roy Castle, worked for many years with his father, attended the same Sunday School and Chapel. When Roy was five years of age, he took part in the Children's Anniversary Service of which I was the Chairman. He was so brilliant that I congratulated him and asked the congregation to give him a round of applause.

ELSA PAGE

Because of illness as a small child our doctor advised dancing and exercise for me. When my local dancing teacher retired I was sent to the Nora Bray School in Huddersfield to learn tap-dancing.

One day a man I can only remember as Arthur came to the class. He wanted a few of Nora Bray's talented youngsters to join his

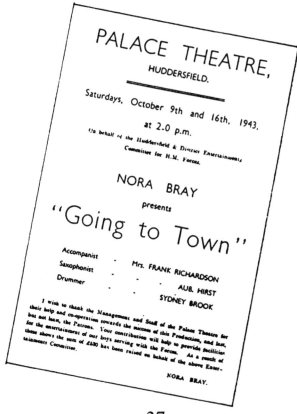

PALACE THEATRE,
HUDDERSFIELD.

Saturdays, October 9th and 16th, 1943,
at 2.0 p.m.

On behalf of the Huddersfield & District Entertainments
Committee for H.M. Forces.

NORA BRAY

presents

"Going to Town"

Accompanist - Mrs. FRANK RICHARDSON
Saxophonist -
Drummer - - AUB. HIRST
- - SYDNEY BROOK

I wish to thank the Management and Staff of the Palace Theatre for their help and co-operation towards the success of this Production, and last, but not least, the Patrons. Your contribution will help to provide facilities for the entertainment of our boys serving with the Forces. As a result of these shows the sum of £630 has been raised on behalf of the above Entertainments Committee.

NORA BRAY.

Concert Party to entertain old and sick people. He took us in a coach to Storthes Hall near Huddersfield to entertain mentally ill patients.

I did my dance and sang 'Oh Johnny' then after me a little boy came on the stage—very small and he had to be lifted on to a chair. I was surprised because I expected him to dance but he sang beautifully. He had fair hair and I'm sure this little boy was Roy.

BILLY SALTER

I always remember this story Roy told on TV some years ago about the day at school he discovered he needed glasses. He sat near the back of class and the teacher was chalking away at the blackboard. After he stopped writing the teacher asked the class a question but Roy couldn't understand the question, let alone answer it.

He was surprised when a boy behind him offered a solution and was amazed when the teacher said 'That's right'. Roy shot round to look at the boy and thought 'Crikey, where did he get that from …? He's a genius!' When other people started giving correct answers to these impossible questions, Roy started wondering what sort of class they'd put him in.

It was only when the lesson was over and he walked past the blackboard that he realized all the answers were written on it, but because of his poor eyesight he couldn't see them from his seat!

JEANNIE CARR

I first met Roy around 1944. We went professional together when we were twelve years old.

While we were at the Queen's Theatre, Cleveleys, we used to see every film—free—during the afternoons. On one occasion I lost ten shillings and I was devastated. I remember sobbing, 'I don't care about *my* five shillings, it's the five shillings I send home to my mother each week!'

A few days later, Roy presented me with a small tin, with two half-crowns embedded in lemonade crystals! Generous to a fault, even then.

HARRY & LORNA MUNCASTER

In the early days of his career Roy Castle often stayed with my late grandmother in her guest house in Cleveleys, when he was in summer season in the town. Granny Johnson came to look on Roy as one of her own family, always talking fondly of him and his mother and she followed his career with pride.

We got in touch with Roy in August 1988, as Granny Johnson was approaching her 100th birthday in December 1988 and, although she was planning her own party, we thought a card from Roy would be a lovely surprise for her. Roy promised he would send a card as he had very fond memories of 'Auntie Bertha in Cleveleys'.

Unfortunately, Granny Johnson passed away in October 1988, after a short illness. Roy sent a lovely letter of sympathy and regret that she'd missed reaching 100. He'd decided to accept our invitation to be a surprise guest at the party!

In 1994, when we went to see Roy at Manchester Arndale Centre on his Tour of Hope, he signed again a photograph he'd first signed for 'Auntie Bertha' in 1948. We shall treasure that photograph and, for us, Roy will never be forgotten.

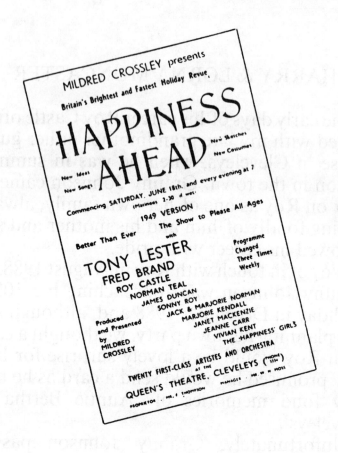

MILDRED CROSSLEY presents

Britain's Brightest and Fastest Holiday Revue.

HAPPINESS AHEAD

New Ideas
New Songs
New Sketches
New Costumes

Commencing SATURDAY, JUNE 18th, and every evening at 7
(Matinees 2-30 d wet)

1949 VERSION

The Show to Please All Ages

Better Than Ever

with

Programme
Changed
Three Times
Weekly

TONY LESTER
FRED BRAND
ROY CASTLE
NORMAN TEAL
JAMES DUNCAN
SONNY ROY
JACK & MARJORIE NORMAN
MARJORIE KENDALL
JANET MACKENZIE
JEANNE CARR
VIVIAN KENT
THE 'HAPPINESS' GIRLS

Produced
and Presented
by
MILDRED
CROSSLEY

TWENTY FIRST-CLASS ARTISTES AND ORCHESTRA

AT THE

QUEEN'S THEATRE, CLEVELEYS (PHONE 1334)

PROPRIETOR : MR. F THOMPSON   MANAGER : MR. W H MOSS

VIVIAN WHITE

Many years ago, when I was a young girl growing up, my father was a stage manager for Northern Theatres Ltd. He travelled the North for them and he eventually settled permanently as stage manager at the Theatre Royal, Rochdale in the late 1940s. I always spent plenty of time around the theatre, as you can imagine, and Roy Castle and the touring company used to play there quite often as the show was very popular.

I remember Roy tap-dancing on the top of a huge drum—so big it seemed to fill the stage—whilst playing the trumpet at the same time. I used to watch him at rehearsals and at the evening shows I was allowed to sit in the wings. I must have been one of his earliest fans.

I hope they have a huge drum in Heaven for him to dance on.

NORMAN TEAL

Roy and I first met in 1946—he was then about fourteen years old—and we were friends for almost fifty years. In the early days, Roy worked for me and my first wife, Mildred Crossley, in a show called *Happiness Ahead* both on tour and in resident summer seasons. We then did a double act touring theatres in England and Scotland, and when he became more famous he invited me on several television shows. We always kept in touch.

In the days of his theatrical beginnings and up to my last memories, Roy was always caring, dedicated and hard working. I was always proud that he thought of me as his close friend and teacher. In one newspaper article he said I gave him a University grounding in show business. Roy's mother also paid me a compliment many years ago, saying, 'If Roy is as good a man as you I'll be very pleased.' In our many years together on tour etc., I feel proud to think that advice I passed on in those early days helped make Roy a good and caring person.

In his very young days his mother asked me to keep an eye on Roy. Later on, when the girls started to chase him, he said he wouldn't bother with them until he was famous—so his friends always said he was more fond of his trumpet than his crumpet!

MARJORIE KENDALL

I first met Roy in 1948 when he was fifteen years old and we were in a show called *Happiness Ahead*. Roy was the star and he used to lead us girls in song and dance routines. The Military Tap routine he did was terrific and always went well, as did the 'Tantalizing Mother' sketch he did with Tony Lester. He used to stop the show singing 'You always hurt the one you love'. The audience loved him.

We certainly had some good times. When we were at Cleveleys, Roy and I used to cycle to Blackpool after the show, leave our bicycles at my aunt's and go dancing to the Ted Heath Band at the Winter Gardens. Dickie Valentine, vocalist and impressionist, was our idol. He helped Roy up the ladder of success later.

We teamed up again with Norman Teal in 'The Norman Teal Trio'. It was with Norman and the trio that we had a spell touring in *Randle's Scandals* with the inimitable Frank Randle. I left the musical act in 1954 to join the Royal Kiltie Juniors, but Roy told me this story of when they played the Wood Green Empire. Frank had been misbehaving himself, as usual, and one day the manager brought the curtain down on him and kicked them out. He somehow got another show in for the following day and when Roy and Norman went along to collect their instruments and costumes, a juggler was established in their dressing-room, almost ready to go on for the matinée. He had a dog which he told them must *not* be let out of the room at any cost.

Well, would you believe it, someone, who shall remain nameless, collected their bits and pieces and 'accidentally' neglected to shut the door as they left. Roy said, 'The dog shot out like it was on a piece of elastic. We could hear "The Ritual Firedance" on the tannoy so we knew the juggler was doing his spot. Suddenly we heard the dog barking, followed by laughter, after which the dog came back to the dressing-room wagging its tail with a juggler's club between its teeth!' They made a hasty exit.

MARJORIE NORMAN BENNETT

My first husband Jack and I first met Roy when we joined the *Happiness Ahead* company in 1949, rehearsing at Elland, Yorkshire. We were all from Yorkshire at that time, Elland, Halifax and Huddersfield. Roy would be about sixteen and a very happy person, always full of life.

Roy had an exceptionally strong singing voice and a brilliant personality. When his voice broke he had a very disappointing time, so Jack and I suggested he joined us in a few comedy numbers. In the Summer Season it was six shows a week, three different programmes, matinée if wet. Roy was delighted.

We were very great friends and during the sunny summer days we used to spend the afternoons on the beach in Cleveleys doing acrobatics—hand springs, cartwheels, balancing tricks. This proved useful later when Roy asked me to choreograph a number for him with 'the girls' because at the end of the number he was at a loss for a good finish. I suggested he finish with a terrific hand spring from the back of the stage to downstage centre. This he did and it was just right.

After I retired from show business I pinned on the wall of my Dancing Studio a photo of Roy taken in Rio and this small photo used to spur me on as I passed it around, dancing in a circle with my ladies tap class. I still have that photo attached to the mirror in my bedroom.

PEGGY SMITH

My husband and I were on honeymoon in Thornton Cleveleys when we went to the Queen's Theatre. At the time Roy must have been only sixteen or seventeen years old, but he was a bundle of energy—dancing, singing, and playing many instruments.

We enjoyed the show so much we decided to go again as they changed the programme half-way through the week. We went to book some seats and—lo and behold!—there was Roy sitting in the box office. The artistes had to take their turn in the box office. We had a little chat with him and after that we watched his progress through the years and always remembered the young boy we knew would make good in show business.

ALBERT CRAN

I was stationed with Roy at RAF Dyce, Aberdeen, between 1951 and 1953. I remember him practising his trumpet—boy, was that noisy! The sergeant who took parade was a Scotsman and always carried under his arm a chanter, which is part of the bagpipes.

One morning Roy was on parade, and asked the sergeant 'What's that you got, Sarge? Could I have a look at it?'

'Hurry up then,' says the sergeant, 'we're running late already.'

By this time Roy is looking it all over, putting it up to his eyes, looking towards the sky. 'What do you do with it?'

'You play it, man! You play it!'

Roy put it to his mouth and had a blow while the sergeant was shouting 'Come on then, come on!'

Then Roy played 'The Cock of the North' just as good as any piper. I tell you, the sergeant was not impressed but, for the rest of the men, you could have heard a pin drop!

HORACE LESTER

I remember the following piece in a Spring Special edition of *Yours*.

'I did not consider National Service to be a particularly funny part of my life,' writes Mr Dillon of Basingstoke, 'but one of the brighter interludes during my "incarceration" at RAF Dyce near Aberdeen, concerned the late Roy Castle. Roy was posted to Dyce as a storeman and seemed to have a lot of spare time to practise his trumpet, which could become a little wearing on the nerves to those in close proximity. So an old trumpet was bought from a junk shop and given a real hammering until the last thing it resembled was a trumpet. Roy's trumpet was then removed from its usual place and replaced by the doctored one.

'Believe me, it almost started the Third World War! Needless to say when Roy realized the joke was on him, he blew his trumpet louder than ever.'

JIM RONNIE

In the early 1950s I was doing part of my National Service at RAF Dyce in Aberdeen and Roy was in the same billet. Many a night he would keep us entertained tap-dancing up and down the length of the hut, up on the table, then a chair, in fact anything he could put his feet on! He used to cut the lads' hair for a shilling, but because we both played the trumpet (our usual number then was 'Charmaine'!) he would cut mine for free. Often in the evening we would practise throwing a cricket ball to each other at the back of the billet as we both played in the camp cricket team.

GEOFF NUTTALL

In the early 1950s I played cricket for Thornton Cleveleys in the Palace Shield league. I usually played for the second eleven and another member of the team was Roy Castle. I would have been seventeen and Roy would have been nineteen or twenty. If we won the toss we always batted first so that Roy was sure to get a bat, because when it came to about five o'clock he would say 'I have to go now, lads' and we carried on with ten men. He had to go early because he was appearing in the Cleveleys summer show.

I recently met another ex-player, Colin Threlfall, who also remembers playing with Roy. He told me that he and his wife would go to the second house of the show on a Saturday night. Roy would see them in the audience, leave the stage playing one of his instruments, walk down the aisle to Colin and, between notes, say quietly, 'How did we go on?', then return to the stage!

PEGGY HUGO

In the spring of 1959 Roy came to Plymouth with the Showbiz XI Football Team to play an ex-Argyle XI at Millbay Park in Plymouth. I remember Jess Conrad was the goalkeeper, Norman Rossington also played and Pete Murray did the commentary.

In the interval, our friend, George, asked if he could bring one of the players home to watch the England v Hungary match on TV. I asked who the player was and my husband said, 'I think the name was Roy Castle.'

'Roy Castle?' I gasped. 'But he's a showbiz star—he made a big hit on the Royal Command Performance a year or so ago—he does everything!' After the match I rushed out to buy extra food and had a steak and kidney pie and veg, fruit salad and cream, ready for when they arrived. When they came in I asked brightly if they would like some pie, only to be told they had had sandwiches at the hotel!

Roy hung back and said, 'Actually Peggy, I could eat something. I finished a stint at Great Yarmouth yesterday, couldn't stop for breakfast this morning before coming to Plymouth and all I've had in nearly 24 hours are the sandwiches.' To my delight he demolished a good meal and two helpings of dessert whilst watching the match which

Hungary won 1–0.

At that time Roy had a programme on ITV called *Castle's in the Air* and I said, 'You know, you'll have to do something on BBC as we don't get ITV here yet, except through Rediffusion.' He was really amazed at that and kept saying, 'I never knew that.' Then he said, 'Funnily enough, I was asked to do a spot on BBC next week. I was going to turn it down because I'm so busy but, just for you, I'll accept it now.'

The following Saturday he appeared on *The Joan Regan Show*, singing, dancing and playing the trumpet.

SIR HARRY SECOMBE

Roy was a very special person in so many ways, a man of such outstanding versatility that you can say of him that he was a jack-of-all-trades *and* a master of them all. A fine sportsman, a dancer, a great singer, a much underrated actor, a tremendous performer on a variety of musical instruments—as I remarked on the occasion of his funeral, if he had taken up embroidery he would have been a record breaker at that too.

Add to all these talents a heart as big as a house, courage in the face of dreadful adversity and you have a most remarkable man who truly justified every superlative I have used.

It was my great fortune to be present at the Royal Command Performance in 1958 when he burst on the showbiz scene and left the rest of us floundering in his wake. I was in the wings, ready to follow him, realizing that it would be impossible to do so until the applause he had generated had died down. He went back three times to take a bow and I had to push him to do so. He just couldn't believe what was happening to him, and the look of wonderment on his face was typical of the genuine modesty with which he greeted the acclaim awarded to his achievements throughout his subsequent career.

We worked together in many shows, including *Pickwick* on Broadway, summer season and pantomime at the Palladium and innumerable television and radio shows.

The last show we did together was a revival of *Pickwick* which opened at Chichester in 1993 and in which he played Tony Weller, the father of the character he had created back in 1965, Sam Weller. Roy had already gone through one course of chemotherapy but he never allowed any of us to feel pity for him. Throughout the rest of the run and the tour which followed, his state of health went through a succession of troughs and highs but his smile and his spirit remained undimmed.

Every night I would bring him forward at the curtain call for a special bow and the audience rose to him in such an outpouring of love that none of us could restrain the tears.

A few days before he died, Fiona rang me at my home in Majorca to say that Roy wanted to talk to me. He wanted to say 'Goodbye' to me before the pain killers that he was taking made it impossible to speak coherently. He told me that he was now ready to go and that I was not to worry because we would meet again.

What a man—we shall not see his like again.

FRANCES WEST

I came across this cutting about Roy and his early success amongst my old recipes.

'We're proud of you, son, but remember, we want the same boy coming home as left here.' So wrote Mrs Lila Castle to her son, Roy, in 1958 after he'd taken show business by storm with a dazzling act at the Royal Variety Performance. She is still intensely, immeasurably proud. 'Roy's success had been a dream of mine ever since he was a little boy. I come from a musical family and I'd have been a professional singer myself if I'd had the chance—but all my ambitions were centred on Roy. And, you know, he hasn't changed a bit—he's wonderful.'

'How could I change with a mother like that?' grinned Roy. 'She's always known what's best for me. She sent me to dancing lessons when I was a boy and I hated them. She said I'd thank her one day. And she was right!'

Mrs Castle and husband Hubert still live in Yorkshire, where Roy was born. But when we spoke to her she was visiting her son and his wife Fiona, and their two children at their home in Gerrard's Cross, Bucks—and preparing one of Roy's favourite meals—meat and potato pie with cauliflower in white sauce, and a choice of apple roly-poly or mint pastie to follow. Recalling his boyhood days, Roy said, 'I adored Mum's meals and the sound of the pudding plop-plopping as it boiled near the open fire was music to my ears—I couldn't wait to eat it!'

DENIS KING

Having spent two years sharing a house with Roy while appearing in summer seasons together at the Brighton Hippodrome and the London Palladium—and enjoying the company of one of the kindest, most generous, and deeply talented people I've ever known—my most vivid recollection of Roy was the first time I ever saw him.

It was 1958, and my brothers and I were asked to appear in our musical trio, The King Brothers, in the Royal Command Show at the Theatre Royal, Drury Lane. I watched rehearsals from the stalls, thrilled, as stars like Pat Boone and the casts of *My Fair Lady* and *Where's Charley?* ran through their numbers.

Midway through the afternoon, there came on stage this very boyish figure wearing thick-lensed glasses and nervously clutching a paper bag which turned out to contain his band parts. Apparently he had spent the previous couple of nights orchestrating the song 'Blue Moon'—typical of Roy. Although not a trained musician he decided he would have a go and had gone to the library and found books on How To Orchestrate. He did it—and surprisingly well too!

He then began to rehearse his act—and I became aware of something very special happening. Suddenly all attention in the theatre was on the stage as the other performers, stagehands and everyone else stopped what they were doing, mesmerized. This small bespectacled figure began to weave his special magic. He told jokes, he played the trumpet, he tap-danced, he sang, he was extraordinary.

Roy became an overnight sensation of course, stole all the reviews, and I feel very privileged to have been there watching it happen.

JOY CLOUGH

In the early 1960s my husband and I went with a group of friends to the Press Ball in Bradford and Roy Castle was there with friends, all of whom were appearing in panto at the Alhambra Theatre.

One of my girlfriends and I were walking down the stairway when Roy, in his wonderfully charming way, swept us off our feet, running down the stairs to open the door for us two 'young ladies', as he called us, and then dancing into the middle of the road for us—it made our night!

BRUCE FORSYTH

I was reading Roy's autobiography and was amazed how similar our careers were—serving in the RAF and the early days of Variety—it's a wonder we hadn't met earlier than we did. Any extra time with Roy would have been a plus. I didn't know that we had both auditioned for the Windmill Theatre; we both admired Jimmy James (a wonderful stand-up comedian in his day) who, like Roy, I would watch from the side of the stage. Roy was lucky enough to actually work with Jimmy, whereas I only had the pleasure of announcing him on *Sunday Night at the London Palladium* some years later.

I first met Roy when a new television show was devised by Brian Tesler called *New Look*, which enabled a lot of young performers to be seen on TV. Roy and I got on straight away, particularly as we were both all-round performers. Rehearsals were fun and Roy's sense of humour combined with my own always worked. They were wonderful days to look back on.

I've said this a few times on TV but I think that it bears repeating: Roy Castle was the most underrated performer in the UK. His massive talent was never recognized in the way it should have been. Why, I don't know—but I, for one, would have liked to have seen more of Roy Castle the Performer.

I remember at the dinner held to mark my fifty years in show business, Roy was one of the speakers. He had only just resumed working after his first illness and he opened his speech by saying 'I'm glad to be here, a lot of people thought I wouldn't be!' I have seldom heard such warm applause and it was a mark of the affection in which Roy was held by all his colleagues.

Forget his enormous talent, he was a wonderful human being and we all needed him to be around for many, many more years. His loss was our loss but his courage and dignity, not forgetting that of Fiona and all the Castle family, was an example to us all.

PAUL DANIELS

One of the most entertaining jugglers in the business was a man called Rob Murray. His skill was hidden behind a stream of one-line jokes delivered in a drawling, slow style. Like most speciality acts, his entire routine lasted around twelve minutes on stage.

When the theatres faded away for variety artistes and were replaced by working men's clubs, Rob Murray got a job at the Cresta Club in Solihull, where he was told that he would have to do twenty-five minutes. Top of the bill was Roy Castle.

Rob explained the position to Roy who asked him, 'It's very easy, can't you pad it out a little bit?' Rob said that he could try.

'What you do,' said Roy, 'is you do your act as per normal and then do it backwards and that'll double your time.'

Rob said he couldn't believe it, so that night Roy went on stage and did exactly what he'd told Rob Murray to do. He went half-way through his time and then started to work the same material—songs, dance routines—back again, making jokes about the fact that they'd seen it before but nevertheless being very entertaining. For the rest of the week, the audiences saw Rob Murray's act forwards and in reverse.

TERRY RUSSELL

One night sometime in the mid-1960s, Roy appeared as the cabaret at the annual dinner and dance of the company I worked for at the Grand Hotel in Bristol.

During a superb performance he was constantly heckled by a lady who had, shall we say, taken more of the amber nectar than was good for her. After showing commendable patience, Roy finally sorted her out with the comment, 'Now I remember you! It was about ten years ago at one of my shows ... I'm not too good at faces, but I never forget a frock.' She was silenced!

ERNIE HILLIER

I am a musician and play saxophone and clarinet. In 1968 I went with my wife to Bournemouth for a week's holiday and when we booked in to our hotel I met Freddy Staff, a trumpet player and old friend, who was playing at the Winter Gardens. He was with the Ted Heath band and they were backing the Tom Jones show with Roy Castle. We went backstage every evening and, of course, we met Roy.

One day my wife and I went to the gardens for a stroll and one of the Scottish regiment bands was playing a lament, with a lone bagpiper coming out of the trees. Now, Roy played the bagpipes quite well and, the same evening, I said to him, 'Roy, I saw your greatest rival today.'

'Who was that?' he asked.

When I told him about the piper he replied, 'Yeah, but I bet he can't tap-dance!'

MARGARET UNSWORTH

Many years ago I was accompanying my husband on a round of golf at the North Shore Golf Club in Blackpool, and as we were unloading the car we met Roy and other well known celebrities who were in Blackpool for the season and had come out to enjoy a game of golf.

I was bored following my husband round, especially when he lost a ball and the fruitless searching in trees and shrubberies began to tire me out. It was then that I saw a ball lying in the middle of the fairway and picked it up. 'Here it is all the time,' I shouted. My husband said that it couldn't possibly be his ball.

Suddenly, Roy came striding into view, looking around and saying, 'I thought that was a good clean hit.' He was mystified—I was for going home—my husband was very embarrassed! We returned to the car after signing out in the clubhouse and I tossed the golf ball into the boot of the car. 'Do you think it was his?' I asked.

'Bound to be, there's no other answer. It's not mine. You should never do that without being sure.'

Roy's golf ball stayed in a wine glass for many years, however, when we learned that Roy was ill, we wrote to him telling him the whole story. We were very pleasantly surprised to receive an almost immediate reply from Fiona, 'Roy forgives you, he always wondered where that ball went!'

The ball is now on show again, shown around with great affection.

JOHN JUNKIN

Touring in *The Odd Couple* with Roy in the early 1970s, we found ourselves in Billingham, where I had booked a room in a little private hotel. Roy, expecting to find accommodation easily enough, came unstuck as the town was hosting a large conference and was booked out. Eventually, my landlady said that she could put up a single bed in my room if we didn't mind sharing, and so it was settled.

After the performance on the Tuesday night we were invited to the inaugural night of Radio Durham, where we duly arrived after midnight and proceeded to make not only fools of ourselves but also a severe dent in a bottle of Remy Martin.

Arriving back at Billingham we crashed out, me in my bed under the window and Roy tucked up in the corner.

What can only have been a couple of hours later I was woken by a train going over a nearby crossing and, as it did so, giving its customary two-tone 'beep BEEEP!'

Now, many people will tell you that Roy was never off. Not through any neurosis, but through the sheer joy of performing.

Early next morning he proved it to the hilt. As the notes of the train died away, Roy carried on in perfect key and tempo; so, to my astonishment I heard:

'Beep BEEEP!'

'... Tonight! Won't be just any night. Tonight there will be no morning star!'

When at breakfast, much later, I enquired, 'Did I actually hear you singing a duet from *West Side Story* with a train this morning?'

He had the grace to laugh.

TOM O'CONNOR

When we think of Roy Castle we remember the man who tap-danced, played trumpet, sang and hosted television shows. We tend to forget that he was also a very fine comedian in his own right. To be able to feed lines to a man of the genius of Jimmy James takes a special talent— and very few possess it. Roy had it in abundance and, to me, was at his best in the comedy mode.

Of all his many stories, the one that still makes me laugh out loud concerns a night Roy was appearing in Geordieland.

Working at a social club in Newcastle, Roy wanted to tell the audience of an experience he'd had at the Savoy Grill, but he suddenly realized they might not know where that was, so he said, 'The other week I was at the Savoy Grill. For those who don't know, that's in London.'

A voice on Roy's right boomed, 'Where's London?'

'Well,' said Roy, 'it's south of Sunderland, I'll tell you that.'

'Where's Sunderland?' came a voice from Roy's left.

'Second from bottom!' boomed a man on the right.

A classic!

III

LOVE AND LAUGHTER

ALEC SWALLOW

Roy's mum was my sister. When she married she lived next door to our Mum and Dad—Roy's Grandma and Grandad Swallow. When Roy was at Scholes School, two of my brothers and I were in our teens and we were all full of fun. As you can imagine we used to join in with his games—and he was full of tricks. We talked to him in a really silly language and called him 'Ricka Raddie', a name he remembered all his life. The silly language was a lot of nonsense, like:

'Where are you going, isn't it?'

'Don't do that, didn't you?'

'It's going to be a good yesterday, wasn't it?'

But he soon caught on to these nonsense sentences and became better at them than we were!

Roy was the only boy at dancing school and he didn't like being with all the girls, but his Mum encouraged him to keep going and in later life he was really thankful. Before attending dancing classes he used to clog dance on the flags outside our houses.

My wife and I were the youngest couple in the Swallow family and when we all went out for the day Roy would always travel with us in our car. He would see a hillside or an interesting stream and say, 'STOP! Uncle Alec, let's get out!'

When we said, 'What about the others?' Roy just said 'Oh never mind them!' He was full of life and far more interested in running up that hillside!

He was also marvellous at bird nesting and trout tickling in our local Morton wood. He was a member of Scholes Cricket Club and a very keen player.

One of my best memories of his success was the thrill of the Royal Command Performance, when my wife and I escorted Roy's mum. We sat in the dress circle about eight seats away from the Royal box, dressed in full evening dress. What a marvellous experience that was. My wife and I had to return up north the next day and poor Roy was left to cope on his own with interviews and photographs. We watched him leave in the back of a taxi—his face was a mix of excitement and sheer terror! We really wished we could have stayed to support him.

After only a short period of genuine 'Star' success he bought his Mum and Dad a little Morris 1000—the registration was KFR ... Roy's parents said it stood for 'Kiss From Roy'.

I have a lot of memories—all of them make me smile. He was a very happy person and it rubbed off on anyone in his company.

DON SMOOTHEY

One of my favourite memories must be our first meeting at the Glasgow Empire in 1957 where I was appearing with my late partner, Tom Layton. I was looking at the noticeboard inside the stage door, checking on times, dressing-rooms, etc., when a voice said, 'Excuse me, are you Don Smoothey?' I turned and said, 'Yes'.

'Well, Dickie Valentine asked me to convey his best wishes. My name is Roy Castle,' he said.

I took to the lad right away. That night he was second spot and as I stood on the side of the stage watching him work, I was absolutely knocked out by his talent. We spent the rest of the week chumming round together. I took him out to Queens Park to play golf, which he was very good at—he beat me every time we played. During one conversation he said he wanted to break away from Jimmy James and be on his own. He said he was going home to see his mum and dad at Cleveleys the next week and I told him to give me a ring if he was ever down in London and we would have a chat.

On the following Thursday I got a telephone call from him to say he was here in town at Richmond station. I went to pick him up and there he was, standing outside the station with a rather well-travelled suitcase and well-travelled trumpet case. When he spotted me his face beamed and he greeted me with that lovely 'Hey, Hi!', like he always did.

My wife and daughter took to him immediately. He stayed a couple of days and then went off with Dickie Valentine to Coventry. Dickie dropped him off at our house the following Saturday night and that was it—he stayed with us for two or three years, on and off, and we had some wonderful times together.

A neighbour of mine taught him to drive on a little dual-controlled Austin A5. Roy being Roy took to it like a duck to water and he passed his driving test at the first attempt. His agent arranged for him to pick up a new car on the Great West Road, a Ford Zodiac, two-tone lemon and grey. I went with him to drive the car back.

We got inside the gates of Richmond Park and changed places. I told him to drive round the park a few times to get used to the car.

Then I got out and he went round a couple of times on his own. After lunch he went off to the Palladium for a matinée show. I asked him to phone when he got there to let me know that everything was all right. Eventually the phone rang and he told me everything was OK but he was soaking wet with perspiration after driving the lovely new car up the Bayswater Road, round Marble Arch into Oxford Circus on a

Saturday lunchtime—it must have been absolutely terrifying!

It was the night of 3 November 1958 that Roy really became a star—the Royal Command Performance at the London Palladium—he stole the show. The following day, the newspapers had photographs of his dear mum and dad on the front pages and the press were chasing him, but, even with all that going on, he found time to come to see me in hospital.

My partner Tom Layton was also visiting me at the same time and wanted to know if I would be all right to appear at the Chiswick Empire later in the month. I asked him who would be top of the bill and he said someone by the name of Cliff Richard. I said I had never heard of him and Roy said, 'Well you wouldn't, you've been in here a month!' That story went round show business like lightning.

Soon afterwards, he had his own TV show *Castle's in the Air* with the King Brothers and Lionel Blair. Then he got his first offer to go abroad, to South Africa, and he asked us if he could have a party. My wife and I said, 'Go ahead, make yourself at home, we rather enjoy a party.'

'Good,' he said. 'I was thinking of inviting you!'

We had a wonderful time, the King Brothers were there, Lionel Blair and his sister, Joyce, Alma Cogan and Dickie Valentine. Everything was going fine.

At about 2 o'clock in the morning the doorbell went and a policeman told me the noise could be heard a quarter of a mile away. I asked him in for a drink and he started to recognize the faces—he was knocked out by all this. After a while he said, 'Excuse me, sir, but I think we'll be all right if you just close the windows.' He intended to make the most of this wonderful experience.

Dickie Valentine, Roy and myself were really very close. There was one time when Dickie and I were in our agent Syd Grace's office. Dick was not feeling too bright and Syd Grace, who was also Roy's agent at the time, said, 'Why don't you boys pop down to the Paris cinema and see Roy? He's doing a broadcast from there today.'

So, we went and, of course, had a nice time and a bit of a laugh and a giggle with Roy.

On the way home we decided to stop and have a drink at the Hare and Hounds. As I said before, Roy beat me at golf—he was also a very good footballer, he wasn't bad at cricket—in fact he was good at everything he touched. After a while, people in the pub started to recognize Dick and Roy, so I said to Roy, 'There's a snooker table round the back here, do you fancy a game?' thinking I must be able to beat him at something.

Anyway we played and I was quite a bit in front until it came to the colours when all of a sudden, bang, bang, bang, the colours disappeared and once again Roy had beaten me.

After a while I felt I had had enough, so I went to get the bus home and left them there. Missing me, they came out just in time to see me get on the bus. They jumped in the car and were waiting at the next stop. They jumped on and told the conductor they were police officers and were arresting me for not having paid for the snooker table! The passengers all looked up, wondering what was going on. They waltzed me off the bus, put me in the car and drove me home. Just typical!

When Roy bought his first house at Sutton he employed a very dear friend of ours to do some extensive alterations. The idea of buying the house was to bring his mum and dad down from Cleveleys. His dad had retired early because of a heart condition and Roy's mum had to keep an eye on what he ate. The house was nearing completion when they moved down, but there was still some touching up to do.

The house had a big double garage and during the lunch break the painter used to sit out in the garage and have his lunch. Dear dad would chat to him while he was having his lunch and sit and eye these sandwiches. After a while, the painter could stand it no longer and asked if he would like one, so the dear old chap dived in. From then onwards, each lunchtime,

Roy's dad would sneak out so that Roy's mum could not see him and have a crafty sandwich with the painter.

It goes without saying that Roy was a great one for charity events and he would do anything, large or small. During the time he was living with me, we used to pop in to one of the locals near my home and have the odd beer. He wasn't a great drinking man, but a good friendship sprang up, and when the landlord of one particular pub was celebrating his twenty-fifth anniversary in the pub he asked Roy if he would come along to grace the celebration and raise money for Guide Dogs for the Blind. Roy not only came along, but brought along his guitarist and pianist and his miniature trumpet. He had also written a special calypso for the evening.

After they sang their song, which was absolutely marvellous, Roy threw a challenge out to the packed bar that he would play any song they named on his miniature trumpet for £1 over the counter for the charity. Well, they shouted and he played and the pounds went over for the charity but quite honestly we had just wanted him to be there to grace the evening.

Roy finished at something past midnight round in the public bar playing darts with the chaps, but they had to put £1 over the counter for every double or treble that Roy got. I can assure you that on top of everything else, he was also a very good darts player! My goodness, they raised some money that night!

In the spring of 1990, Joan Savage along with the BBC Concert Orchestra were doing a broadcast from the Golders Green Hippodrome. She had Roy as her guest star. She invited my wife Joan and me along without telling Roy and there was a little reception afterwards. When he saw us he greeted us with the normal 'Hey, Hi!'

Afterwards, we were having a little chat and I asked him if he could be at our golden wedding anniversary on 9 June. I knew that Joan would be over the moon if he could be there and he said he would do his best and asked what we would like for a present. I told him his being there would be present enough. He said he would like to do something and asked if I thought Joan would like to go on a cruise. I said it was something she would absolutely love. Anyway that was that, the evening came to a close and we saw him off in the car.

A few days later he telephoned and told me that he and Fiona had booked us a two-week Mediterranean cruise on the *Canberra*—and that I wasn't to tell Joan. What can I say?

The day of the party arrived and at about 9 o'clock in the evening Roy came walking through the door and Joan's face lit up. He had come all the way down from Huddersfield and he handed Joan a large envelope which I think she thought was just a wedding anniversary card.

After the hugging and kissing—she was truly delighted to see him—I said I thought Roy would like her to open the envelope. At first she thought it was some sort of brochure but looking closely she saw that it was tickets for the cruise. She just welled up.

We were to sail on 2 September which was Joan's seventieth birthday which Roy, of course, had worked out. When the day duly arrived, both he and Fiona came to see us off, and on the *Canberra* we had a lovely cabin and there was a bottle of champagne waiting for us. It was absolutely marvellous.

On a sad note, four years later, on the same day, 2 September, Fiona telephoned Joan around 9.30 in the morning to say that our beloved Roy had passed away. I could tell many more stories about this lovely man whom we like to think of as the son we never had.

MARY CORBRIDGE

As near-neighbours of Roy when he lived in Sutton, Surrey, my parents and I were fortunate enough to get to know him as well as his wonderful parents and his delightful wife.

At the time we met the Castle family my father had had several strokes and was partially paralysed. He could not get around very easily and we had no car. Roy's father used to come from time to time and cut my father's hair, but on one occasion he had to miss. Imagine our surprise and delight when Roy turned up instead. He reminded us that this less publicized talent as a barber had been the means whereby he was able to buy his first trumpet.

GRAHAM STARK

A few years ago I wrote a book about my friend Peter Sellers. Fortunately well received, it was the special edition, printed in Braille for the blind, that delighted me most, with a sad reservation. It could, obviously, never utilize the photographs that were in the original book which included the one, taken by a self-timer, of myself sitting in the centre of the vast collection of camera equipment left in my care by Peter Sellers while he went to New York to make a film.

This Aladdin's cave of satin chrome and lenses was mine to use as I saw fit (all eighteen thousand pounds worth), which is a long-winded way of explaining why I was able to attend Roy Castle's wedding at St James's Church, Gerrards Cross, on 29 July 1963 with the Rolls-Royce of cameras, the Hasselblad, dangling from my neck. Adopting a Quasimodo shuffle (the camera was supportable but the equipment bag over the shoulder gave me a Tower of Pisa slant), I tottered among the wedding guests, pointing the interchangeable lenses at all and sundry. The best man (then plain Harry Secombe before the sword walloped the shoulder padding) got the treatment, as did Eric Sykes. Faced with this magnificent camera (typical of

Sellers it was the most expensive in the world), Eric was not to be outdone in the gamesmanship stakes and nonchalantly posed leaning on the door of his enormous Bentley Convertible.

Tri-X film churned through the camera and with a paparazzi use of the elbows, I fought my way through the expectant crowd to catch pictures of the beautiful bride through a swirl of white veil. Lurking at the edge of the graveyard, a firm tree branch to steady the elbows, I caught a lovely, formal picture of Roy proudly displaying his beautiful bride Fiona, just after the ceremony. I felt sure I had a record of a happy day, but there is an infallible rule in photography: the best shots always come at the end of the last roll of film.

Sure enough, with one unexposed frame left in the camera back, I came on Roy, standing by the transport that was to take him and his bride off on their honeymoon. Aptly, knowing Roy's sense of humour, this was no white Rolls, no gleaming garish Cadillac, not even the Sykes Bentley Convertible, just a plain, black Ford Popular with the standard, going-away-on-honeymoon car accessories: tin cans, old hats and clipped-on rolls of toilet paper. Who says the British are not an elegant race?

I indicated there was another shot to be taken. At once the lovely clown face went into a puckish grin and without a pause we got the pose that said it all: pride and delight at a deed well done. A deed that was to stand him in good stead for the rest of his life. There sits Roy with tins of Heinz Baked Beans and Libbys Whole Kernel Corn at his feet, about to ride off with his beautiful bride.

I have a set of favourite photographs I have taken throughout the years and this is certainly one of them. I treasure the delight, pride and happiness on Roy's face.

The real tragedy of Roy's death lies in the simple fact that we can't really afford to lose people like him. A consummate entertainer whose abilities were apparently unlimited, he had the rare quality of arousing not the slightest envy, or jealousy, in any one he ever worked with. After seeing him dance to perfection, sing like the clichéd angel, blow a trumpet like the other angel, Gabriel, and hold his own in comedy—working with one of the greatest, Jimmy James—one could have every reason to secrete a little poison in the heart. But not with Roy.

Many years ago I did a three-handed, one-hour TV show with him and Cleo Lane. An odd trio, but it worked a treat. Smooth and sophisticated, we performed in front of a packed studio audience at ATV Elstree for all of eight minutes, when came the ominous entrance of the studio manager on to the set, earphones clamped to his head, manic twitch to the eye, and shirt-sleeved arms waving madly. As there was no part written in the scene for a shirt-sleeved studio manager, plus earphones and manic twitch, we presumed, quite rightly as it happened, that all was not well.

In those early TV days breakdowns were, unfortunately, rather frequent, and this was a lulu. There was, apparently, 'a slight technical problem', and the studio manager ordered us to 'keep the audience entertained'.

Well, if there had to be a breakdown luckily Cleo and I found ourselves in the company of Roy. A tour de force then took place and for over one and a half hours the three of us kept the audience seemingly quite happy.

Naturally Cleo sang, Roy sang, and I, sensibly, kept my mouth shut. However I was able to join Roy in the dancing and all three of us adlibbed comedy routines.

The studio manager, twitching even more alarmingly, kept assuring us the slight technical hitch was still slight and Lord Grade, at the back of the control box, cigar clenched in mouth at an alarming angle, jetted clouds of smoke that would have done justice to an Apache sending off signals that John Wayne and the Cavalry were on the way. Finally, someone found the right piece of Sellotape and stuck it all together, the floor manager made the masterly understatement, 'Nothing to worry about any more,' and we were able to finish the show. Cleo, Roy and I often laughed

BRENDAN McCUSKER

I was working as a musician in the house-band at the High Post Hotel, near Salisbury in 1976 when Roy appeared there in cabaret. Many bands, comedians, singers, performers and the like played there at that time and they invariably stayed overnight in the hotel during their stint. The after-show atmosphere was usually raucous, riotous and well lubricated!

What struck me about Roy (apart from his usual impeccable and professional act, always rapturously applauded) was the fact that he went home after the show. Even finishing his act after midnight, having quite a long drive, and having to be back at the High Post again the following evening, he always went home to his family.

It sounds simple and trite, but in the heady showbiz atmosphere of debauchery and selfishness prevalent at that time, I found his desire to return home each night refreshing, touching and genuinely to be admired. And I've never forgotten it.

DOUG ROBLOU

A friend of mine told me the following story about Roy and it always makes me smile. One day he was out shopping when he saw a lady sitting in a parked car turn down the window, empty out an ash tray and then close the window again.

Apparently Roy pulled up some nearby turf, walked to her car, tapped on the window and, when the lady opened it, said to her, 'As you left us a souvenir of your visit I thought I would give you a memory of our village!' He then dropped the turf on her lap! She was really outraged, but shortly afterwards her husband turned up, recognized Roy and they all ended up laughing about it. But Roy had certainly made his point.

IAN HALLIDAY

Some years ago my wife and I went on a long weekend holiday to the Isle of Man. While we were there we decided to see a show. The star that evening was Roy Castle.

During the performance he asked members of the audience if they had any particular songs they would like him to perform. One of the audience requested 'Danny Boy'. He duly performed it and finished his performance to a standing ovation.

Many months later we read an article in which Roy told of his son having a serious accident on the Isle of Man. Apparently his son, Daniel, had fallen off a rocky ledge and the day of the accident was the day we saw Roy at the theatre.

As he said in the interview, of all the songs to be asked to sing on that evening, it had to be 'Danny Boy'. His son was lying seriously ill in a hospital bed. He said it almost brought him to a standstill. But he carried on. Just as he did right to his untimely end.

DOROTHY THOMPSON

My sister-in-law lived in Huddersfield and was very proud of Roy who, she said, 'always kept his feet on the ground'.

Some years ago we took her to the Palladium when Roy was appearing there. After the show we persuaded her to go around to the stage door. She was a bit apprehensive having never done that kind of thing before. When Roy came out he stood and chatted with her after she said she was from Huddersfield. Then she said, 'My neighbours will never believe this.' Roy promptly took her programme and wrote across it, 'To prove t' others they were wrong'.

This is only a simple thing but he made an OAP the happiest person around, it also proved she was right about Roy.

DOROTHY LILIAN ANDY

I have a memory I have treasured for years. My sons were very young and Roy was on television, talking about a house he'd moved into and about his garden, in which he was growing vegetables. His face glowed with pride and pleasure as he talked. Someone had told him that if, when he cut a cabbage, he made a criss-cross cut on the remaining stump, he would get more little cabbages. He had done this and he was bursting with pleasure—he'd got the little cabbages. He didn't cry, 'I've made a fortune', no, he'd got this little reward for trying. I've never ever forgotten his pleasure!

When I was a little girl, my mum showed me the same thing, I don't think it meant much to me at the time. Seeing his pleasure made me feel I had learned something too.

DEREK HAMER

Over the years both my wife Vera and myself have seen Roy, who was an old friend, in a wide variety of venues ranging from the Alfresco Pavilion at Sunny Vale Pleasure Park to the London Palladium, but wherever the venue and whatever the circumstances there was always the same warm and genuine welcome.

This was never better illustrated than on one occasion when I was on business in Blackpool. I discovered that Roy was appearing at the ABC theatre and, of course, decided to go and see the show and pop round to see Roy later.

Several of my colleagues decided they would like to see the show too and because there were six or seven of us I decided not to phone Roy to suggest that we meet. As the gang walked up to the booking office a voice said, 'Hey up, kidda! Why didn't you let me know you were coming?' I explained that I was with a crowd and right away he invited us all backstage after the show.

All my friends were entertained and made to feel welcome and at ease and, as we left after about three-quarters of an hour, they all said that they felt as though they had known Roy all their lives.

That's the sort of man he was—a 'grand lad' as we say in Yorkshire.

CONNIE WOMERSLEY

In 1973 my husband, Harry, was the Chairman of Bradford Northern Rugby League Football Club. The team had got through to the final of the Challenge Cup Competition at Wembley—a great occasion for the Club—and Harry arranged to take the boys down to Maidenhead to prepare for the match. They were also invited to a Civic Reception by the Mayor, and Harry asked Roy if he could spare the time to join them at the Reception. Of course, Roy said yes.

Unfortunately on the day the team coach was an hour late arriving and, when they finally met the Mayor, Roy was lying on the floor at his side with an empty glass in his hand, pretending to have drunk too much whilst waiting for them. This gave the lads a good laugh.

Because he supported Bradford Northern then, the supporters of the club remembered this and we collected a record amount of money for the Cause for Hope at one of the recent matches.

BERYL SANDERS

My husband Geoff was performing with Roy in Sweden. Fiona and I were also there with the children and we all shared a large flat. Outside there was a sandpit which the children loved. When they came in there was always sand on the floor and, although the maid came with the flat, Fiona and I liked to clean the sand up before she came in. As we did not have any cleaning materials we sent Roy and Geoff to buy a squeezy mop.

As our knowledge of the language was nil, Roy was put in charge of finding the right phrase and getting the mop. It was a difficult phrase, but he eventually learned it and off he and Geoff went on their mission to buy a 'grubbler'.

The shop assistant could not understand a word, so Roy did the full miming act, together with noises, to the amazement of everyone in the shop. The assistant looked at him and eventually said in excellent English, 'These crazy English! You mean a mop.'

Roy had looked at the wrong word and we never did find out what a 'grubbler' was.

MIKE CRAIG

For me and my family just two words are all that are needed to remind us of Roy—*love* and *laughter*. He overflowed with both those priceless possessions, giving and receiving both all his life. To know Roy was special enough, but to write for him and produce programmes with him was the big bonus. We were both lucky enough to be born in the West Riding of Yorkshire, a fact which prompted Roy on many occasions to say with a knowing nod, 'we understand'.

Roy's sense of humour was very special to anybody who knew him. We were very much on the same wavelength in this respect. I can't ever remember talking to Roy without us laughing. We had a mutual friend who, I suppose, was a modern day Mrs Malaprop. His verbal gaffes were all recorded in a book which Roy kept and when a new malapropism was uttered he would be on the phone to share the laugh. There were dozens, but we had our favourites. One of the first I heard was when we were in Barnsley and this friend was staring at the massive slag heaps around the pit areas. 'Just look at those,' he said. 'They're real sore eyes.'

I can't describe the feeling inside as Roy and I just looked at each other!

I remember Roy ringing me one night with a beauty which had just been delivered. Roy had been performing at a big charity function. The friend had been at the 'do' and proudly told all and sundry how Roy had raised enough money to train 'two blind dogs for the Guides'!

Our favourite has to be this same friend recounting a conversation he'd had with his wife after an evening watching television. He said, 'The other night me and the wife were sitting at home *burning the midnight fat . . .* and we both agreed that Bruce Forsyth had *shot his chips!'* You just can't write lines like that!

Naturally, during the nine years Lawrie Kinsley, Ron McDonnell and I wrote *Castle's in the Air* we had love and laughter in plenty. The rehearsals should have been recorded. With Eli Woods, Mike Burton, Jacquie Clarke, producer Jim Casey (the son of Jimmy James), pianist Brian Fitzgerald and we three writers, it often took two hours to get through the first readthrough!

The thing we all looked for in every script was the line, or even just the word, which was going to corpse Mike Burton. When Mike Burton's sense of humour was tickled by something, he became incapable of reading the line without collapsing into hysterical laughter. The more 'takes' he did the worse he became. Well, when *The History of Corpsing* is written, there has to be a place in it for one of Mike and Roy's longest corpses. There's no question that it should be in the *Guinness Book of Records* and I'm happy to say I have a recording of it! It took them *seven minutes* to get one line out without bursting into uncontrollable laughter!

It was the opening Jimmy James type sketch we always did with Mike, Eli and Roy. Each week Eli would be trying something new—escapology, mind reading, swimming the channel—this particular week Eli had taken up pearl diving. With all the usual build up and enthusiasm, Mike would assure Roy that this was 'the big one'. I quote from the script ...

ROY: Come on then, don't keep me in suspense any longer, what's this new hobby he's got?

MIKE: Pearl divin'.

ROY: Pearl diving?

MIKE: Pearl divin'. He was watching the telly last night when on comes *The Undersea World of Jack Custard*. Well, it came to him in a flash. No one has ever been pearl divin' in the Leeds and Liverpool canal!

ROY: True. That's a fact that wouldn't occur to many.

MIKE: So, if no one's been in there divin' for pearls—it hasn't been played out has it? It must be full of 'em!

... and that was it. Not hysterical, I agree, but

103

Mike Burton could not get through those few lines without collapsing into laughter which, as we all know, spreads like wild fire, affecting everybody else, audience included. Once Mike went, Roy went with him!

All afternoon we had trouble getting through these lines. There was absolutely no way the actual recording would be any different. I can see Roy now as we approached the, by now, dreaded lines. His shoulders were going up and down, he was forcing his lips together in an attempt to stifle the laughter which was building up inside him. And then it happened. Mike got to the line, 'pearl divin'' ... and he just went. When I say 'went' I mean he just *exploded* with laughter. Roy followed. The audience was about five seconds behind them. I have never seen two grown men standing facing each other on stage and just laughing and laughing and laughing as Roy and Mike did that night. Within a minute everybody in the building, the audience, the BBC commissionaires (not noted for their sense of humour), the engineers in the box ... *everybody* was laughing hysterically. What made it so bizarre was that nobody knew what they were laughing at. Basically everybody was laughing at everybody laughing. It went on and on. Jim Casey tried to get them to do one line at a time with the other one off the stage so as not to put the other one off. No chance. Every attempt to calm down and come up with a solution was met with a wall of laughter.

On the night it took seven minutes to record those few short lines. Seven minutes of side-splitting, tummy-aching laughter ... *and we couldn't broadcast any of it*! It meant nothing to the listener, nothing at all, but if you ever see Mike Burton just say to him, 'Tell me about the time you told Roy Castle about Eli going pearl divin',' ... and stand well back!

In October 1993 I asked Roy to take part in an hour-long radio tribute to his mentor, Jimmy James. The programme, called *The Comedian's Comedian*, was recorded in front of an invited audience at the City Varieties Theatre in Leeds and the audience gave Roy a welcome none of us will ever forget. He delivered the most famous of all stooges' opening lines from off stage—'Are you putting it around that I'm barmy?'—and when he walked on, the Yorkshire audience responded.

Recalling that wonderful two-year apprenticeship at the side of the 'master', Roy paid tribute to Jimmy James, saying that one of the most valuable things Jimmy had taught him was 'repose'. He also retold the dressing-room banter which Roy and I have often quoted to each other. Jimmy James had his own code for communicating with his two stooges, Eli and Roy. If a dressing-room visitor had outstayed his or her welcome, Jimmy would get up, move to the door and say, 'I'm just going to check the hamper!' This meant, 'I'll be back in five minutes and he or she has to be out of the room!'

Another favourite, and one that Roy and I used in many situations was, 'This lad's tall enough to be a policeman!' Although it might seem like a compliment, what it really meant was, 'This chap's a bit of a prat!'

But the story Roy told which stole the show took place when Jimmy, Eli and Roy were working at the Bristol Hippodrome. Normally Roy would do his own spot with the trumpet as well as the stooging, but top of the bill this particular week was Kenny Baker, the brilliant trumpeter, so Roy's trumpet was out. However, although he couldn't play it in the show, he did practise up in the dressing-room and on about the Thursday Jimmy James got a message sent up to Roy which was supposed to be from the manager. It said, 'Could you ask Roy to stop playing his trumpet as Kenny Baker is worried that people might think it's him!'

What a guy. Never, ever would he be tall enough to be a policeman ... and that's from a Yorkshireman, and *we understand!*

IV

STAR QUALITY!

FRANCIS ESSEX

By 1965 Roy was in great demand by television producers although he was not yet a 'star' in the full sense of the word—mainly because he always remained 'good old Roy just turning up for work'. I was working for Scottish Television in Glasgow and my wife Jeanne and I had recently moved into a new house, when I invited him to feature in the first of our *Man Behind the Star* series. As further persuasion, I promised him he would be well and truly treated as a STAR.

I met him at the airport and drove him to our house to stay for a week. That evening our newly installed central heating system nearly did for us all. It was one of those gas affairs which was supposed to pump hot air from floor vents in every room, except on this occasion it seemed to pump out pure gas. We heard an explosion, and within minutes Roy was in the cellar, crouching amidst dust and concrete, torch in one hand, spanner in the other, attempting to diagnose and rectify the problem. He was gone for ages. Then, suddenly, every vent in every room became a loudspeaker as he found the hot air duct and stuck his head into it to broadcast, 'I always wondered what it was like to be well and truly treated as a star!'

Roy guested for me in the television series I produced for Millicent Martin. The show's dance routines were set by Paddy Stone, far and away the finest choreographer in the country at the time. I asked him to come up with something brilliant for Roy and Millie, but he pulled a face and grumbled 'but he's nothing more than a hoofer'. Two valuable rehearsal days passed whilst Paddy stubbornly worked with his dancers on the major routine until eventually I insisted he concentrated on Roy's spot. He crossed the rehearsal room floor and looked down at Roy seated in a chair. 'What do you want to do?' he asked curtly.

Roy looked up. 'Learn something,' he replied.

It turned out to be one of the best routines Paddy ever gave us.

BARRY CRYER

'See a pin and pick it up and all day ... you'll have a pin.' That was over thirty years ago and was spoken by Roy at the London Palladium. We'd met through our mutual friends, the King Brothers, and immediately hit it off. Then we picked it up and hit it off again.

During one of my frequent bouts of unemployment—there wasn't much call for comedians from Leeds who thought they were Terry-Thomas—Roy asked me to be his dresser. Typically, he made the request as if he was asking *me* to do *him* a favour, when he knew full well I was out of work.

The professional association was a happy one—except possibly for the night when I went out with the Kings, with Roy's car keys in my pocket. He tracked me down in a club and instead of firing me, turned the whole thing into a joke. Only a couple of years ago, I made it up to him, by walking on stage, waving car keys at him.

Also characteristic was his endless self-deprecation. He used to love to tell the story of how he once appeared at the Theatre Royal, Stratford East and, as he walked on the stage, a man from a box greeted him warmly and enquired after his wife Fiona and their children.

111

A man in the circle shouted, 'Shut up! We want to hear him, not you!' There then ensued an argument between the two, with Roy, as he said, standing silent and watching the debate, like a Wimbledon umpire. During a brief lull, Roy said to the audience, 'You don't need an act from me!'

'You haven't got one!' said a man in the front row.

He certainly had. He was so versatile, his little finger went solo. I used to say to him, 'Is that all you do, those eleven things?'

I can't think of him without smiling, or more often, laughing. I hope you've still got the pin, Roy.

ANTON RODGERS

The outstanding memory I have of Roy was in Detroit in 1965, when we were in America on a pre-Broadway tour of *Pickwick*. The night we opened, I threw a small dinner party in the hotel where we were staying and after we had finished the meal and were relaxing over a postprandial brandy, one of the group of three musicians who were wandering around asking everyone for requests came up to our table and singled out Roy, asking him what he would like them to play. From the top of his head he said 'Tea for Two'.

They started to play and—you have to take my word for it—suddenly we were in the middle of a magical experience, because Roy started to do 'scat' singing to the accompaniment of the three musicians. As if on cue, everything in the restaurant stopped (and I'm talking about 50 to 100 people). I can only liken it to one of those Hollywood movies where suddenly the unknown artist excels himself.

As soon as they had finished 'Tea for Two', everyone in the restaurant applauded and the musicians were begging for more. Harry Secombe, who was at our table, just smiled knowingly, as he had obviously experienced it before. Afterwards, when I asked Roy why he did not do this more often, he just said, 'Anton, I could never make a living out of it, I just do this for my own and my friends' pleasure.'

This happened thirty years ago and in a way I suppose it illustrates Roy's immense popularity within the profession. I loved Roy dearly, even though professionally our work was very different. I have to say his courage did not surprise me at all. It was merely another mark of the man.

DES SUMMERSGILL

During the late 1960s, Roy appeared at the Floral Hall in Scarborough in celebrity concerts. These shows were always a sell out and Roy, billed as 'Britain's Sammy Davis Jnr', certainly gave the audience full value for money with his outstanding talent and enthusiasm.

The one thing he lacked was any concept of time, and because in those days many people had to catch the last bus home, a number of people had to leave whilst Roy was still in full swing. He would often accompany them to the exit and play 'God Save the Queen' on his trumpet as they left!

At one point he told the caretaker of the theatre to leave the keys and he would lock up!

MARGARET HAYWARD

The elder of my two daughters is disabled and attended a school for disabled children near Watford. Every year the PTA (of which I was Chairman) arranged a money-raising fête. One year (I can't remember when, as my daughter is now thirty years old!) we were lucky enough to have Roy to come along and declare the fête open.

When he arrived, looking tanned and healthy having been on holiday, I asked him how much time he could spare us. He said he had about forty-five minutes—and stayed for *two hours*!

When he was eventually ready to leave I walked with him to his car, which was parked a little way from the school. On the way, walking in front of us were two ladies who had attended the fête. We could hear their conversation quite clearly, which went like this.

'It didn't look like him did it?'

'No, he was sort of coloured.'

'Yes, *and* he wore glasses, he doesn't wear them on the telly does he?'

'I wonder if it was really him, or someone taking his place?'

By this time we had reached the car and I was apologizing to Roy for having to hear this conversation!

'If that's the worst I hear about myself in my career,' he replied, 'I won't have done too badly!'

BERNARD CRIBBINS

I've got a lot of memories of Roy because we go back an awful long way—we used to play cricket together many, many years ago—I've got very happy memories of that. He also played golf for me on my charity golf days several times, but one thing we always did have a great laugh about was something that happened on a TV show we were doing—I think it was a Spectacular and we had a sketch to do.

Roy was sitting at a cocktail bar in evening dress, dinner jacket, tie undone, very relaxed, obviously in the early hours of the morning, nice smoochy music, and he is sitting there on a high barstool. He started to sing, 'It's a quarter to three, there's no one in the place, except you and me' and at this point my character, the barman, pops up from behind the bar and says, 'Excuse me, sir, you're not allowed to sing in here, we haven't got a licence, no singing' and pops down again.

Roy then starts to sing again—and this was the whole premise of the sketch. It was very, very slight indeed, and we just could *not* get through it without laughing, and we laughed and laughed for two days in rehearsal. When it came to the day in the studio, we *still* could not get through it without laughing and the producer, Alan Tarrant, came down from the control box and gave us both a terrible shellacking.

He really did have a go at us because we were behaving like silly schoolgirls, sitting there with eyes watering, legs crossed, and we couldn't explain why we were laughing because we didn't know, but we just could not get through it. In fact the only time we did get through the whole sketch without laughing was on the recording in front of the audience that same evening.

That is just one of my happiest memories of a lot of very happy memories of Roy.

WILLIAM MILNE

For long an admirer of the formidable talent, versatility and genial personality of Roy Castle, I was privileged to be present on an occasion when he demonstrated his quick thinking, imperturbability and generosity of spirit to a fellow—if inadvertent and unlikely—performer.

Roy and his troupe were the featured artistes at a cabaret in the Officers' Mess at RAF Strike Command Headquarters at High Wycombe one evening in the mid-1970s. They were performing in the dining-room in an arena formed by the packed crowd, many of whom were seated on the floor. Roy had enthralled everyone with his comedy and instrumental flair and had moved on to tap-dancing while playing his trumpet.

Suddenly there was a flurry from that part of the crowd reclining near the servery. Women leapt to their feet with mild screams. The perpetrator was an enormous and clearly terrified cockroach, perhaps drawn by the Pied Piper playing of our hero. The beast scuttled into the centre of the arena where Roy played and danced on, albeit with a quizzical eyebrow raised.

Recognizing the cockroach as an aspiring multi-legged hoofer, Roy jammed his trumpet over it and conversed with it through the mouthpiece! This calmed and delighted the audience, and apparently also the cockroach. Roy then resumed his playing and tap-danced his fellow performer off the floor and back to its kitchen refuge. The ensuing applause was tremendous.

Afterwards, several of us spoke to him. He was as witty and gracious off-stage as he had been on. Much of the conversation was about his family to whom he was clearly devoted. There could have been few present on that memorable evening who were not captivated by the talent and charm of a very rare artiste and palpably decent man.

TOM WALKER

Some years ago I was on a P & O cruise ship with Roy Castle who headed the entertainment staff.

Roy, in his wisdom, decided to play for the crew against the passengers in a game of cricket. I arranged it so that I could bowl to Roy when he came in to bat—but not with the ball! I surprised Roy by bowling a large, rosy apple which he struck in the middle of his bat. The apple shattered and covered him in apple and juice. Roy chased me all over the ship but he never did get his own back!

TERRY MARSDEN

In 1973 I was given the task of organizing the Chipping Sodbury Lions' annual charity dinner-dance and cabaret. I selected the prestigious Connaught Rooms at the New Bristol Centre and with help from a friend in London successfully booked Bob Miller and his Millermen, featuring Don Lang of *Six Five Special* fame, vocalist Colin Anthony and cabaret entertainer Roy Castle.

I had the very small task of compèring the evening and met Roy for an informal chat prior to his show. Although this was a long time before he became a national television personality, he was nevertheless well known in entertainment circles as one of the best cabaret acts around. I remember him as relaxed and modest of his many talents, and I believe this was about the time that he was involved with the TV show *Castle's in the Air*. I remember discussing this with him, and we agreed that the show did not provide a real showcase for his style of entertainment. He mentioned opportunities in America, but had firmly decided, for the sake of his family, to concentrate only on the British market.

The evening started with dancing to Bob Miller and later there was a cabaret spot from Colin Anthony. At this point I was called to the door where a young Irish 'gatecrasher' was asking to see Roy prior to his spot. He explained that he had just completed an act at the Bristol Hippodrome as a stand-up comic and on hearing that Roy was appearing, asked if he could meet him and perhaps do a 'turn'.

After a lot of Irish blarney, I eventually took him backstage and introduced him to Roy, they had never met, and I asked Roy if he would mind if this Irish comedian did a short 'warm-up' spot before he went on.

'What do you do?' asked Roy of this cheeky comedian.

'Oh,' he replied with a twinkle in his eye, 'a spot of tap-dancing, I play the drums, the trumpet, and tell jokes.'

'Really?' said Roy. 'Perhaps I should go on first and warm *you* up!'

It was agreed that the comedian should introduce Roy, which immediately deprived me of my claim to fame! He was very funny, pure Irish wit, and of course did a far better job of introducing Roy than I ever could.

Roy started his act, it was pure magic! The routines were original and funny, and the tap-dancing was full of energy and vitality. He did a drum spectacular with a number of floor tom-toms which was unbelievable, I have never seen anything like it before or since, and I am certain he never performed it on television. A routine with a balancing ping-pong ball brought the house down. Throwing the ball into the air, Roy would catch it on the tip of his nose and then balance it whilst tap-dancing. He would remove it, throw it into the audience and invite the catcher to toss it back, whereupon Roy would again catch it on the tip of his nose and run about in a show of mock balancing. It looked impossible, but he did it every time. Later, he told me the secret, 'Just spread a liberal amount of clear glue on the end of your nose.' So simple and yet very effective. I wished that I had been left with the illusion. Although I must admit that this later became my party piece!

The evening was a huge success, Bob Miller and his band, Don Lang and Colin Anthony all provided great entertainment, but Roy Castle was outstanding and his act became the talking point for many a month after. Seeing him later as he became more popular on television I believe his real talents were never truly exploited, but perhaps this was how Roy wanted it, this was certainly the impression he left with me, modest and content, he didn't want anything greater other than to simply entertain.

I did get to introduce the Irish comic. 'What name shall I say?' I asked him. 'Just announce Jimmy Cricket,' he replied!

ROGER HOLMES

In August 1973 I was on holiday with my parents and sister in Dorset during Corfe Castle Carnival. All the local villagers and holidaymakers were awaiting the big parade, which was to be led by Roy Castle. Suddenly there was a cloudburst over the Purbeck Hills. Seeing everyone getting soaked, Roy climbed to a vantage point and played 'It ain't going to rain no more no more'. The rain stopped, a rainbow developed, the sun came out and the sky was blue once more.

ANN BOSTON

My friends and I have very fond memories of two wonderful tap-dancing lessons with Roy Castle. We had hired a minibus to take the fourteen ladies who belonged to our tap-dancing class to the London hotel where Roy had his studio. On arrival, he greeted us as if he had known us all our lives. We were a very mixed bunch of ladies aged from 30–65, and with *very* mixed abilities!

He treated everybody the same and took a great deal of time and effort to teach us a dance that we could all do. He even invited the man who had driven us down to London to join in and, much to his amazement, proceeded to stick taps to the bottom of his shoes. Roy also took a lot of time and care with the older ladies. How did that man smile all the time? I don't think we stopped laughing once.

RAY CAMPBELL

I am the leader of a dance band and we were so lucky to work with the great Roy Castle several times.

On one occasion at the Crest Hotel, Crowborough, in the late 1970s, Roy was in the middle of his act and had just got to the bagpipes routine when a Scot yelled out, 'I bet you canna play "Amazing Grace"! I bet you £5.00 you canna play "Amazing Grace".'

Roy said, 'Right, you're on!' and prepared to work up plenty of air.

He was just about to start when the Scot followed up with '... to my satisfaction!' Roy collapsed into laughter and the entire room joined him, it was several minutes before he could continue.

Another time, Roy asked if he could borrow one of our boom microphone stands and I lent him mine. This was on the first night of a five-night run. Roy was singing 'Georgia' and then went into his trumpet solo—just as the boom arm of the stand started to sink to the floor. Roy did not miss a note but followed the microphone all the way to the floor and hit the last note flat on his back. Brilliant, just brilliant!

I apologized to Roy and assured him I'd lend him a different one for the remaining nights.

He said, 'No, don't do that. I want to do the same thing every night.' But, would you believe it, we couldn't make it happen again!

COLIN JONES

I first met Roy in the lounge bar of the George and Dragon hotel in Baldock, Herts. It was a Sunday lunchtime about twenty years ago, and Roy and a friend called in for a drink. They were en route to Yarmouth, where Roy was doing a one-night stand on the pier. I was with a gang of friends, about ten of us, standing at the bar quaffing and telling gags.

Roy was laughing along with the rest of us, and eventually it came to his turn. He started off by saying that he couldn't buy his personal number plate RC1 as it belong to the Catholic church. Max Bygraves had sold his to Mercedes Benz for £10,000 and Val Doonican wouldn't have his at any price!

In due course we all went home happy and Roy's joke duly did the rounds locally. It was some six years or so later that I next met Roy.

By this time I was working as a patrolman for the Automobile Association, still in Hertfordshire. I came across Roy broken down on the A1(M) near Stevenage. Roy remembered me and the time at the George and Dragon. We started trading jokes as I mended the car. On completion of the repair I went to my van and brought out my trumpet, which I used to play while waiting for calls.

'Do you want me to play for you?' said Roy.

'No,' said I. 'I'll play, you dance.' To my dying day I'll never forget the huge smile on Roy's face as he tap-danced and I played 'Sweet Georgia Brown' on the hard shoulder of that busy motorway. As he left Roy said, 'You've made my day.'

As far as I was concerned, it was certainly the best tip I'd ever had.

PETER CHAPPELL

In 1979 I was a serving officer in the Gwent Constabulary and an active member of the Gwent Police Choir, which had been asked to perform a charity concert with the Thames Valley Police Band at The Hexagon, Reading, to be compèred by Roy.

The curtain went up to a full house. After the usual preamble and pleasantries, Roy introduced the choir. 'The only Welsh Choir I know without a "Jones" in it!' he announced. Absolutely true! He had obviously done his homework.

Opening the second half, he dropped what the choir could only have described as a bombshell. Crossing the stage to talk to our Musical Director, he asked him, with the microphones live, 'Do you think that your boys could sing "Bye Bye Blues"?'

'It's not a part of our usual repertoire,' replied the perplexed MD. 'But yes, I think we can manage that.'

'Well done,' enthused Roy, 'because I am now about to become the only entertainer in the world to tap-dance the accompaniment to a male choir.'

Nobody in the theatre that night could possibly have known what was going to happen, except I suspect Roy himself, but less than five minutes later, without any warning and obviously without any rehearsal, the audience erupted and brought the house down on an impromptu item that stole the show.

Only Roy Castle with his confidence and strength of character could have pulled off a stunt such as that. Truly a memorable occasion.

CHARMAINE FLETCHER

Between June and August 1988, Roy starred in the definitive programme about the Salvation Army, Anglia Television's *Marching As To War*. The programme was a celebration, in music, drama and song of the life and work of the Army's founder, William Booth. A great story, it took another great man to tell it and that is where Roy stepped in.

On one occasion, Roy was filming in Switzerland, where William Booth's daughter, Kate, was imprisoned for her religious activities, in the castle of Neuchatel. Music is important in Salvation Army worship, so salvationists always warm to fellow musicians—and none more so than the multi-talented Roy. What better gift could they present him with then, than an Alpine horn?

Given his ability to get a note out of anything, Roy was keen to play it but, ensconced in the small, thin-walled room of a modern hotel, Roy's problem was where to practise playing the huge instrument. Inspiration dawning, he took the horn out into the cool, fresh air of its Alpine home. There, amid the mountains, Roy gloried in its deep resonance, so fittingly rich against the giant backdrop of the Swiss Alps.

As a devout Christian, Roy Castle was a

friend to the Salvation Army, and in turn, the Army was a big fan of his. Thanks to Roy, thousands of people were able to share in its history and work.

T JOHN FOSTER

In 1982 Roy starred in a theatre show with a difference and made over thirty sparkling performances to more than 20,000 Motor Show visitors at the National Exhibition Centre.

This was a record breaker in more ways than one. Live theatre had never been permitted before at this venue, so permission was given with some reluctance by the organizers. Roy was to host and star in *Play Your Part*, an hour-long audience-participation show staged thrice daily in a specially built 500-seater theatre on behalf of the parts and accessories division of Peugeot Talbot. He took to the challenge magnificently, helped all of the other performers and made my role as producer a lot easier.

The semi-final eliminator game involved a mini motorbike and Roy wore a bright red safety helmet. He had performed the routine at least a dozen times and always generated strong laughs. The biggest response came in the show where inspiration struck hard. Dressed in a light-coloured sweater and red helmet, he suddenly turned his back on the audience and shouted, 'How's that for a big Swan Vestas!'

ERIC ROWAN

When I joined *Record Breakers* as the 'new boy' to produce the *seventeenth* series, it was with some trepidation. After all, it was very much *Roy's* show and he was famous for his incredible all-round talents—and for being professional to the core. So there was a lot to live up to. However, he could not have given the new members of the team a bigger or more generous welcome.

Kind, patient, and totally committed, he was also exceptionally brave when he was attempting world records. I vividly remember standing with him on top of Blackpool Tower before he embarked on the world's longest ropeslide. Ahead of him was a 500-foot drop to the promenade below. He hated heights and his face was taut with grim determination. But he had said he would do it and there was no way he was going to turn back. As a Royal Marine commando launched him down the rope Roy even whistled and sang!

He was always utterly honest and easy-going. At the end of each series we used to have the same little chat, which became something of a ritual. I would ask him whether he would like to stay on for the next year, and he would say with his characteristic modesty that he wouldn't like to outstay his welcome. Maybe, he thought, we were after someone younger.

Try as I might I was never sure I convinced him how much we all really did want him to stay!

His determination not to allow his cancer to get in the way of his work was an inspiration. He did not complain and he did not make a fuss. But he still demanded the best of himself and took every opportunity he could during *Record Breakers* recordings to warn the children in the studio audience about the dangers of smoking. 'Don't get like me,' he would say.

A few weeks before he died we spoke on the phone. It was in his words an 'eyeball to eyeball smiling handshake'. He wanted to express what we both already knew, that despite our hopes he would not be well enough to do the next series, but that he was happy to see it go on.

'I want *Record Breakers* to be a good show,' he said. 'I don't want any moping or sadness, that wouldn't be any good at all.'

Then he added, with words clearly chosen with care, 'A gentle bow out would be rather splendid.'

NORRIS McWHIRTER

During the twenty-two years that Roy presented BBC television's *Record Breakers*, there was the occasional item that proved beyond the capacity of even the largest of TV Centre's eight studios—the cavernous Studio One.

Such an occasion arose when the show's first producer, Alan Russell, decided to stage an event for troupes of young tap-dancers from schools of dancing all over the Home Counties. They converged on TV Centre to be led in mass unison routines by Roy, the world's fastest and most durable exponent of their art.

The day came with coaches filled mainly with young teenage girls filling the car parks and side roads. To milk the occasion of every dramatic camera angle possible, Alan had ordered the rigging crew to position a high camera, suspended on a wire pennant, vertically above the great circular courtyard in which the routines would be staged.

The noise of the drilling for the two masonry bolts was too much for the sixth-floor bureaucrats. Roy and Alan were in a planning session in Alan's office when the door burst open. An irate, iron-grey-haired, thin-lipped female administrator of uncertain age, but close to her indexed pension, stood there quivering with indignation. Looking up from their table, Roy and Alan heard her deliver what became a BBC classic: 'Anyone might think,' she hissed, 'that this place was built for entertainment!'

CHERYL BAKER

I remember when I was asked up to the BBC for an interview regarding co-presenting *Record Breakers* in 1987. My first thought was, 'I wonder if Roy Castle is as nice in real life as he is on the television?' (Funnily, since I started on the series, this is the one question that everybody asks!) Anyway, he was just as nice. I was obviously nervous, as I really wanted the job, but Roy had a wonderful gift of putting people completely at ease. At the end of my interview with Eric Rowan, the Executive Producer, I felt as if I had known Roy for years. He was very comfortable to be with.

I learned such a lot from Roy. That wonderful ability to make people feel confident when minutes before they had been quaking in their boots has, hopefully, rubbed off on me in some small way. It was great fun working on the programme with Roy. We used to laugh a lot, especially at some of the stranger record attempts, but I think Roy enjoyed his little acting roles best of all. When he was dressed in a cowboy outfit, sitting on top of a bucking bull holding his hat on and singing at the same time, I really had to bite my lip to stop laughing.

There was another side of Roy that people did not very often see. He always put such a brave face on especially when he was attempting records. Remember, his records included parascending under ten London Bridges, wingwalking for approximately three hours and twenty-three minutes and a ropeslide from the top of Blackpool Tower to the promenade below. All this, and yet Roy had a dreadful fear of heights. He was very clever at disguising his fear with laughter but a trembling lip never fooled anyone!

My memories of Roy are too great to recall in just a few words—I feel privileged to have worked with such a talented man, who, first and foremost, was a warm hearted, generous human being.

CELIA TRURAN

I was staying at Park House on the Sandringham estate the day Roy and the BBC were filming the world record attempt for the longest conga. Moving around the field to see what it was all about, not having seen *Record Breakers* before, I stopped to talk to Roy. He said, 'Come on, join in!' I declined, I'm a pensioner and didn't fancy doing the conga around the vast area of Sandringham Park.

'My family wouldn't believe I'd done it,' I said. But Roy was very persuasive, 'Come on, you can do it,' says he. 'Dance the conga for me and I'll sign your programme to prove you did it.'

Now, never say die's my motto, and before you could say 'Roy Castle' I joined hands and I did it. I was number twenty-eight in row twenty-four and I have Roy's autograph to prove it.

I had a lovely day, met a lovely man, have a lovely memory. What more can I say!

GREG CHILDS

Roy was a person who lit up a room. Whenever we went to film *Record Breakers*, people would approach him and talk to him as though they'd known him for years. Sometimes it would get quite confusing. We'd ask, 'Was that an old friend?' and he'd say, 'Oh no. They just wanted a chat.'

But that was his way.

I remember once we filmed a gigantic orchestra—a thousand children all playing music together in a park in Cambridge. Roy played too, of course, and at the end of the event, as the organizers and dignitaries packed up to go, the kids wanted Roy's autograph. So we formed a queue, a thousand people long, and he signed every one individually and chatted to them too. It took hours.

During his illness Roy turned up at Earl's Court for the first ever indoor Aerobathon. People from all over the country had gathered to exercise together to raise money for charity and try to break the record for the world's largest Aerobathon. When Roy went on stage to announce the result, there was an outpouring of love and respect which took everyone by surprise—especially, of course, Roy. Out of the blue and with one voice the entire crowd of over thirteen thousand sang his

144

song, 'Dedication', back to him. This was the song he had sung to them in over twenty years of *Record Breakers*, at the end of every show. Now they were paying him back with an enormous, spontaneous, collective 'thank you'. None of this was stage-managed in any way, but, as he left, the crowd parted quite naturally to let him through, producing an apparently endless corridor of well-wishers applauding him and shaking his hand. I remember thinking that no one could ever have experienced a more heartfelt and moving ovation.

It was a hero's exit, and he deserved it.

KRISS AKABUSI

It was my great privilege to join the *Record Breakers* team in the last eighteen months of Roy's life. Obviously, a man of that considerable talent had much to contribute to my learning experience in the entertainment business.

Two things he said have remained with me. Firstly, you need to be able to know the difference between light and shade. When I first came into show business I was full of energy, excitement and enthusiasm and I threw all of it at the camera continually, for the whole show. Roy said that the public would not appreciate the high times unless you showed them the low times.

The other thing that Roy told me was that in between shows and when the camera was not running I would have to go to the dressing-room and recuperate for my next performance. Roy is not gone, he is just recuperating while the angels wait for his next performance.

TOMMY STEELE

The meeting had to be secret! We both knew it: if the word got out that Roy and I had met, then showbiz would know that the casting of Cosmo Brown in *Singin' in the Rain* was executed at last. And from that news, the inevitable question would come: 'Is Castle going to do the famous wall flip in the number "Make 'em Laugh"?'

We decided to have our chat on neutral ground—somewhere quiet, somewhere safe—somewhere so remote that discovery would be impossible.

'Beaconsfield!' Roy suggested. 'I know a little tea shop in the middle of the tiny village. I'll get there first at 4.00, if the coast is clear, I'll sit by the lattice window with my back to the street—then you can come in safely.'

And so it passed.

We sat snuggled together chatting about the coming musical at the London Palladium. Roy was thrilled to be offered the great role created by Donald O'Connor but, like me, was anxious to bring to his performance the dreaded wall backflip.

'I won't do that part, Tom,' he insisted. 'Not unless I can crack the flip.'

I nodded, wondering if he shook inside, like I did, when I even *thought* about such a stunt, eight times a week—LIVE. No camera, no rest, no retakes. Every night *up* the wall, *over* the ramp and *crash*! on to the hard stage.

'Can you do it?' I ventured.

'I can,' he smiled. 'But I'm not sure about these.' He indicated his knees knocking under the table. 'But I'd like a crack at it.'

He went on enthusiastically about a troupe of acrobats that could teach him the basics. By the time the third pot of tea had disappeared, we had agreed. He would spend two months with the acrobats and at the time he considered right, I would come and see the flip—or *not* as the case may be. We shook hands and, with our collars up around our cheeks, crept towards the exit.

It was obvious to both of us that announcing Roy as the actor in the show and then him having to admit he couldn't do the flip would be disastrous. The agreement we had made that day would protect us both. Thank Heavens we had used our brains and met undercover.

Roy reached the exit just before me. An elderly lady suddenly reached out from behind a stack of cream buns and swung them around. She stared hard at both him and me and muttered to her companion, 'I was right, Rose. That's two of 'em—you look out for Debbie Reynolds while I get the umbrellas.'

Footnote: Roy cracked the flip and he and I

played in *Singin' in the Rain* at the London Palladium for two and a half years. The elderly lady and Rose were never seen again!

played in *Singin' in the Rain* at the London Palladium for two and a half years. The elderly lady...

GERALDINE CAMPBELL

Whilst I was in London some years ago for a short visit, I went to see Roy and Tommy Steele in *Singin' in the Rain* at the London Palladium—an absolutely terrific performance. Afterwards, I went to the stage door in the hope of seeing Tommy or Roy. After a while Roy appeared. He took time to talk to everyone and sign autographs. I asked him if he would mind if I had a photograph taken with him. He readily agreed. I happened to pass a remark that I would have loved a photograph of Tommy, but he said that Tommy wouldn't be out for quite a while, 'but, if you trust me with your camera I'll go and take one for you,' Roy said. Trust? I was absolutely delighted. Off Roy went with my camera.

When he returned, another young girl asked if he could explain how to do a particular step. He did better, he began to demonstrate down the street. I carried some papers for him whilst he did this. After he had demonstrated the steps he turned to me and said, 'If you send me the photographs, I shall have them signed for you.'

He was true to his word and I treasure the two photographs—signed personally to me.

He was an inspiration to lots of people and

will be sadly missed. His giggle, his smile, the twinkle in his eyes, his gift of making everyone feel at ease. A truly genuine and sincere Christian man.

A C ROBERTS

I went to see Roy and Tommy Steele in *Singin' in the Rain* at the London Palladium. It was a superb show, with Roy in a very demanding role. Afterwards, we went to the stage door for autographs and there was a group of schoolchildren and their teacher. It was after eleven o'clock at night when Roy appeared and the first thing he did was to ask if they were the children from such and such a school. He then said, 'Which one of you is Richard? I hear you enjoy playing the cornet.' He took the time to have a long chat with Richard and the other children and was genuinely interested in hearing what they had to say. I thought it was wonderful that, tired as he must have been, his first thought was for those children. I felt that was typical of the man.

TONY BURWOOD

For the greater part of the 1980s, I was the licensee at the Coach and Horses in Great Marlborough Street, London W1, and Roy, who was in *Singin' in the Rain* at the Palladium, was one of my customers.

I first met him when he came into the bar late one night, after the show. As was our custom, and our instructions to the bar staff, we pretended not to recognize celebrities. We worked on the theory that our customers were entitled to a quiet drink; if they wanted to introduce themselves or talk we would take our lead from them.

Roy wanted to talk, and our conversation that first night was confined to the show, but as we got to know each other better we swapped family stories, we talked of our ambitions and our hopes for the future.

I was saddened by Roy's death, but I was not surprised at his determination to fight his illness. Despite that boyish, irresistible grin, I knew the man had backbone: he had previously stood by my side and helped me out of a very sticky situation.

When Roy came into the pub after the show each night, we were getting ready to close. The customers, who had packed the place during the day, had long since taken their trains back

154

to the suburbs, and the bar was nearly empty.

It was on such a night that trouble entered in the form of four young men in their early twenties, bent on confrontation and destruction, they were looking for any excuse for a row. Roy stood by my side as we both reasoned with the youngsters and finally talked them out of the pub. After they had gone, I told Roy he had been silly to get involved. He could hardly work the next day with a broken arm or two black eyes.

'That's what friends are for,' he told me. I found this very touching, but then he went on to tell me of his battle plans. 'I had my loose change in my hand,' he said. 'I was going to throw that in their faces first, and then, in the confusion, hit them with the soda syphon!'

So much for his boyish, cheeky grin!

I have plenty of Roy Castle stories to tell, but none show his generosity more than the day he pretended to be a close family friend to help out my youngest son.

My two sons went to school in Essex, and the younger, Matthew, was always boasting to his friends about the mysteries of living in a Soho pub. Such was his bragging that he was almost expected to produce a new marvel every day. Stuck for a fresh idea, he told his astonished friends that Roy, who was admired by the kids for his work on *Record Breakers*, was a close family friend. Unfortunately he was unable to back his claim up with any firm evidence and his friends were beginning to doubt his story.

My wife told Roy about Matthew's predicament, saying that he had two school friends staying for the night. 'If I call them down,' she asked, 'would you just say hello?'

'No, I'll go up,' replied Roy. 'Where are they?'

Although he had never visited the flat Roy strolled into our lounge as if he was a constant visitor. Sitting down on the settee he asked Matthew, 'How did we do with that homework I helped you with?' He then spoke to the young visitors at length about school and finally excused himself, saying, 'I was really looking for your Dad, he's not downstairs. Would he be in the office?'

Matthew said later that the whole time he was in the lounge, Roy acted the part of a family friend or uncle and fully convinced the gobsmacked schoolboys of his friendship with our family.

Needless to say, Matthew's reputation at school was enhanced.

My family is a little richer for the time we spent with Roy, and I am very proud to have known him.

PATRICK MOWER

Roy and I lived quite near each other in Gerrards Cross, and when Roy was starring in *Singin' in the Rain* with Tommy Steele, I was starring opposite Susan George at the Apollo Theatre in Clifford Odet's play *The Country Girl*.

We both had a three o'clock matinée on a Thursday and we would often catch the same train from Gerrards Cross Station. Our respective shows had been running for a few months and one lunchtime, on arriving at Marylebone Station, I saw Roy across the platform and called: 'Roy! How do you fancy having Susan George this afternoon?'

Roy turned, put his hand on his hip and said, 'No thank you, Patrick. I'm quite happy with Tommy!' He did a little pirouette, blew me a kiss and waltzed his way off the platform!

The two o'clock train from Gerrards Cross will never be the same without him.

TREVOR HOOPER

In October 1987 I was invited to attend a retailers convention in Portugal. Whilst waiting for my flight at Luton airport, who should I see but Roy Castle. He was quite alone and I thought to myself 'If I get back home and I tell my family I have seen Roy Castle and not spoken to him they will never forgive me.'

I introduced myself to Roy and he was just wonderful, asking what I was doing and about my family. Amazingly, it transpired that Roy was also going to the Convention as 'Top of the Bill' at the Night Club nights.

Fancy Dress was required for these nights and, being a big Al Jolson fan, I did the full thing and donned black suit, black wig, white gloves, black tie and of course black face for my first evening. Roy saw me and, like he did with many others, had a chat about my outfit and suggested I join him on stage at the end of the next Night Club evening. He wanted me to sing, live! After a lot of talking with Roy and with my colleagues pushing me very hard, I finally agreed. I would do two songs only, 'Swanee' and 'Mammy'.

The big night came and at 1.15 a.m. I was pushed, shoved and carried on stage after Roy's signal to my friends. He gave me a microphone and said, 'Just start singing and

158

we'll follow.'

I started with 'Mammy' and Roy and his band just came in and helped me to sing with more confidence. I felt fine and the audience applauded. We then went straight into 'Swanee'. With Roy's help I felt much better and enjoyed the second song even more.

Applause came and I then went to hand the mike back to Roy because I had done my two songs. To my amazement the audience wanted more. Roy said, 'Stay on! Stay on! What other Jolson songs do you know?' That for me was wonderful because I had done my two songs and Roy was 'Top of the Bill'. He could have said, 'Thanks, Trevor' and got me off the stage having done my bit. But no—Roy encouraged me to stay with him and I was on stage for another half hour. It was a once in a lifetime experience and I will always remember Roy for being so generous to me, for giving me a taste of show business and a night to remember.

SYDNEY GARNER

Although it is now sixty-five years since I first started in show business, apart from occasional passings in a corridor or sightings across the platform at Crewe Station, Roy and I met only once—but that was memorable. He was just about to finish in pantomime at the Pavilion, Bournemouth, and I was opening in a new play at the Palace Court. For reasons which escape me, we were both invited to attend a civic lunch at the Town Hall and, presumably because two 'actor chaps' might be expected to know what to say to one another, we were seated together.

It was one of those occasions of municipal pomposity and we started to fall apart with laughter when two robed dignitaries somehow got their chains of office inextricably entwined. By the time the Lady Mayoress had dipped hers in her soup, we were both dangerously on the edge of hysteria. We continued to deteriorate throughout the meal and when the speeches followed and the Town Clerk, by misplacing a page of his notes, produced the astonishing statement that 'the sad death of the Inspector of Weights and Measures was the result of a sterling effort by the Bournemouth Police Bank', we lost control completely and helped each other from the room.

As well as having that happy, personal memory to keep by me, I have always felt that Roy represented a standard of integrity in his professional and private life which not enough of us try to emulate and I can say with honesty that I never met anyone who did not feel the same way.

PATRICIA DAVIES

About twelve years ago, my husband and I went to our local theatre to see Roy. The announcer made the introductions, Roy walked on to the stage and the audience erupted. The expression on his face was one of sheer bewilderment, and when the applause had died down he said, 'Who did you think was coming on?'

This to me portrays Roy's continued surprise as to why he was so popular; when in fact it was due to his modesty and his down to earth nature, that people loved him so much, apart of course from his many talents.

PAT HUDSON

I have sung traditional jazz for many years now and about ten years ago I was singing with Harry Long's Good Time Band at The Fleece at the village of Addingham. In those days the band played in the tap room, which was always packed, and one night my husband and I went into the lounge bar to buy our drinks before the show. A friend of mine said casually, 'There's Roy Castle playing with your band tonight in the tap room.'

'Oh yes?' I said. 'And I'm Queen Elizabeth II.'

Much to our amazement as we pushed our way in, there was Roy belting out a tune in his inimitable style.

After a while, Roy announced over the mike that I was going to sing. I went up to the band and was greeted by his usual beaming smile and a kiss. I sang 'Won't You Come Home Bill Bailey' and 'I Can't Give You Anything But Love', at the end of which on the last chord I sang 'If you want to be a record breaker—yeah!' Roy, laughing pretended to hit me on the head with his trumpet, but I got another kiss.

I shall never forget that night and Roy's willingness to let a stranger sing with him. His warmth and smile were very genuine and I'm

very proud to have had the opportunity to sing
with him.

SIR BOBBY CHARLTON

I was taking part in a promotional event with Roy at Warwick University a few years ago. We were talking about motivation and I told him about my work with children and how I like to keep their attention and make them laugh with magic tricks.

He then went out of his way to show me a new trick that I could use. It was done with shoelaces, working them in such a way that they appear to get into a terrible mess, then—Hey Presto!—it all comes undone!

He even gave me the words to use and I still use them and the trick with the children. The way Roy took the trouble to teach me that trick showed his generosity, unselfishness and willingness to help other performers.

MAUREEN LIPMAN

I had always wanted Roy to play opposite me in *Wonderful Town* and was disappointed when he couldn't do it. He was such a good actor as well as a complete all-round entertainer and I was such a fervent admirer of his that I felt we would have worked terribly well together.

Years later, I was throwing a surprise party for the eightieth birthday of the mother of composer Denis King, at my house in Muswell Hill. Denis and Roy had known each other well when Denis was one of the King Brothers and Roy had often spent time in the company of Denis's mother and father. We were thrilled when Roy and Fiona came to join the party and it really made Win's evening. During the course of the party I told him how disappointed I'd been that he couldn't do *Wonderful Town* and his dear face looked even more disappointed than mine. He hadn't known anything about it and said he would have loved the opportunity as much as I would.

At that time he had already had treatment for cancer in its early stage, and at the party he made us all roar with laughter by telling us of the letter he had received from a woman who had written that she was so sorry and that 'It couldn't happen to a nicer fella!'

Dear Roy Castle. He may be gone but he'll always be with us.

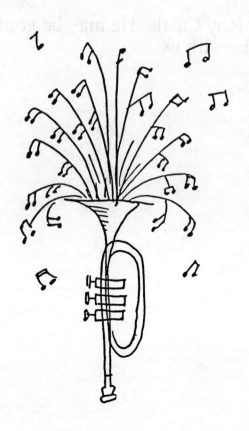

ROGER POOLE

As Chairman of the Wolverhampton Christian Aid Committee, I wrote to various celebrities in 1993, asking them to support our project, Challenge '93 'Trees for Uganda' Appeal. I invited sketches (on postcards) of trees, so that these could be auctioned at the special fundraising evening held in November of that year.

I suggested that the celebrities might, if they wished, sketch a tree in a way which reflected their personalities or interests. Roy certainly did that and his was by far the most original.

HENRY COOPER

I will never forget two outstanding occasions—firstly, when Roy and I performed a speech together with Roy dressed up as a Guardsman, which was a very humorous routine and secondly, when I last saw Roy a few weeks before he died. I was taking part in a golf day in his honour and he made a point of thanking each celebrity who had come to play, even though he looked exhausted. He made such a wonderful effort to ensure that everyone felt so very welcome.

HOWARD PARKER

As many people know, Roy was a great admirer of Stan and Ollie for many years and did a more than acceptable impersonation of Stan Laurel, usually with Sir Harry Secombe as Oliver Hardy. I was delighted when he agreed to become an Honorary Member of the Laurel and Hardy Appreciation Society Hats Off (Derby) Tent, of which I am Grand Sheik.

My memory of Roy Castle is when he starred in a one-man play called *Stan Laurel* in August 1991 at the Theatre in the Forest,

Grizedale in Cumbria—just a few miles from Stan Laurel's hometown of Ulverston. In it, he played the parts of Stan's father 'A J', Fred Karno, Hal Roach, Stan's lawyer, Oliver Hardy and, of course, Stan Laurel. He was on stage for well over two hours—acting, dancing, singing, playing the trumpet and tap-dancing! He played all parts brilliantly—when he portrayed Stan in old age, it was as though it *was* Stan himself.

I once asked Roy which was his favourite Laurel and Hardy film and with his reply came the illustration on the previous page.

HEATHER QUINN

I have a particular memory of an interview Roy gave some years ago. When he was asked by the interviewer what was one of his proudest moments, he told the tale of when he happened to be staying at the same hotel as two of his greatest heroes—Laurel and Hardy.

He said there was a knock on his door one night and when he opened it, there stood Stan Laurel and Oliver Hardy carrying a huge book full of famous autographs they had collected over the years. They went on to say how honoured they would be if he added his name. He said he felt so proud and it was a most wonderful night.

ROY SAUNDERS

Twenty-five years ago I opened my morning paper and there on the second page was a photo of Roy Castle and Janet Webb sitting on a bench dressed as Laurel and Hardy. I was amazed at Roy's likeness to Stan Laurel.

At the time, I was in a comedy group and we did a Laurel and Hardy sketch in the act. I thought how great it would be to do a sketch with Roy. But I knew I was only dreaming and that it could never happen, so I forgot about it. But my wife never forgot.

I had been a fan of Roy's for years because the stage is in my blood. My father and mother met on the stage when they both worked in Variety. Mother was a dancer in the chorus and my father had a five-piece Dixieland band and also appeared in sketches with some of the old stars. Roy worked with the same stars years later, people such as Jimmy James, Albert Modley, Jimmy Britton and Dougie Wakefield.

Unbeknown to me, in January 1990, my wife and daughter wrote to Cilla Black at *Surprise, Surprise!* to ask if I could do a sketch with the great man—my wife had never forgotten my dream. Cilla asked me to come down to London and do my Oliver Hardy impersonation for her. I said yes! So my wife and I went to London and were made most welcome.

The next day we went to the studio to meet Cilla and rehearse. Cilla told me she would be playing Stan's part, we rehearsed the sketch about three times, then they said it was OK. I couldn't help thinking while in the dressing-room before the show, how perfect it would be if Roy could have been there to do the sketch with me, little knowing he had been in the studio all the time.

I was introduced to the audience the first time, had a little chat with Cilla and then went off to change into my Oliver outfit. When I came on the second time to do the sketch, Cilla was still in the same clothes. I thought to myself, when is she going to get changed?

When I sat down next to Cilla she said, 'I've had a word with your wife, Ray, and I wasn't your first choice for Stan, was I? Now, be honest, who would you *really* like to be Stan in the sketch?'

I thought to myself she didn't say that in rehearsals, then I said, 'Roy Castle.'

'Well Surprise, Surprise!' said Cilla. 'You wanted the best, we got the best! Come in, Roy!' It was wonderful. As soon as I saw him coming down the steps towards me, my nerves went away and I knew he would pull me through the sketch. It was the greatest time of my life, and after the show we went to the hospitality room for drinks. Roy stayed with us and we talked about our families, he was very proud of his wife and children. While we were talking, a young lady came up and asked Roy what time he would like his car. Roy said, 'I'll go when Ollie goes.'

Roy had a warmth about him, as soon as we met he made us feel like old friends.

In 1991 LWT asked me if I would work with Roy on *You Bet!* I couldn't believe my luck, it was great to work with him again, he made things so easy it was a pleasure. Roy Castle was not only one of the world's great entertainers, he was also a gentleman.

Yes, dreams can come true. I will never forget him.

V

CURTAIN CALL

PENNY TREBLE

Hope Castle

Roy laid down the foundations
As he lived life with a flair
He built it up, brick by brick,
By showing he did care.

How could he know that cancer
Was waiting in its lair?
And when it reared its ugly head,
Roy laid his feelings bare.

His final work inspired us
He showed a courage rare
When, through his private suffering
He still found time to share.

And who could not be moved to help
When our lives we compare
To the man who smiled, and waved with
  hope
As he struggled from that chair?

I hope he sees, from where he is,
That people do still care
And knows we're not just building
Castles in the air.

ANN DUCKETT

Although I was never actually introduced to Roy, he was directly responsible for bringing me back into the Church.

One day my friend said Roy Castle was coming to St Peter's to talk about his cancer and his faith, so I agreed to go. It was a wonderful service with Roy playing his trumpet with his sons, Benjamin and Daniel, on their instruments. First of all Roy spoke, and then Fiona. I was very moved. The service was videoed and shown on two later dates in the coffee lounge and I was so impressed that I went to see it again.

When my friend asked me if I would like to go to the service the following Sunday, I readily agreed. That was two years ago and I've been each week since, even being confirmed.

I know if it hadn't been for Roy I would never have gone, but he was such a wonderful man, I shall be for ever grateful to him. Going back into the Church has completely changed my life.

PASTOR JIM GRAHAM

Roy was baptized as a believer by immersion in water in our church some months before he died. For many years he had played the trumpet and led the brass section in our church orchestra. We had kept his baptism a closely guarded secret for fear that the media might want to parade it. Roy never wanted his spiritual life to be trivialized but that it would have dignity and reality and credibility.

When the time came for him to be baptized in our Evening Service, he simply stepped out of the orchestra and into the baptismal pool. His family (three of whom were in the orchestra) had moved to the other end of the pool to receive him after his baptism. The orchestra was seriously depleted. So Roy, dripping with water, led the family back to the orchestra and joined them on his trumpet to lead the evening congregation in closing worship.

BRUCE GRANT-BRAHAM

Roy and Fiona Castle touched our lives when they visited our local church a few years ago.

We live within sight of the church, and Roy and his family were staying at their seaside holiday home nestling in the pines just a short distance away. The family regularly visited the area in high summer and every August Roy would lead the Family Service on one special Sunday. The particular occasion I remember was when our oldest daughter, Danielle, was asked to read the lesson when she was only about nine years old.

It was obviously very intimidating for a youngster to be asked to read in front of a packed church, let alone with a celebrity she 'knew' well from *Record Breakers* sitting in the pew just in front of her. To say that she was nervous was probably an understatement.

Danielle arrived a few minutes early for the service with her younger sister, Anika. Her mother, Barbara, and I were trying to be supportive and to stave off stage fright. The four of us found ourselves almost alone in a deserted chancel along with Roy and Fiona. Having introduced ourselves, Roy immediately felt Danielle's concern and put her at ease with a few kind words. 'Are you nervous?' he asked her. 'So am I. My knees are knocking together under these trousers but we'll help each other, won't we?' The two then started to chat as if they had been friends forever.

From that moment on Danielle was given a huge inner confidence as his kindred spirit egged her on when it came to her turn to stand in front of the microphone and to read to a church that was by now bursting at the seams. He looked her between the eyes throughout and her reading went perfectly.

I have since met a large number of celebrities—all with different personalities. None were like Roy, though. He was special and I shall never forget how he selflessly went out of his way to make one little girl's day. She is now fourteen and to this day his photo and autograph hangs on her bedroom wall.

KATH HOWATSON

In 1980, a close relative of mine died from a malignant brain tumour. She had four children, the youngest only six years old. For the last ten days of her life she was in a coma and my husband, his brother and I spent those ten days taking turns to sit with her day and night.

Immediately after her death we decided to go away for a few days, being both physically and mentally drained. We arranged for the children to be cared for by relatives and made our way around the country stopping at various places.

One day we stopped for lunch at a roadside pub miles from anywhere. There were a few people at the bar but no one in the room we went into. We were waiting for our meal to arrive when three or four casually dressed men came into the room. My husband said he was sure one of the men was Roy Castle. Being from Huddersfield, Roy's home town, my husband couldn't resist going over to him and striking up a conversation. Roy was so pleased to hear we were from Yorkshire and we spoke about various local places known to him and about the old days in Huddersfield.

He was so genuinely friendly and amusing, none of the 'I'm the big star' attitude. We had never met before but it was just like meeting an old friend we hadn't seen for years.

He asked why we were in that part of the country and jokingly asked if we were lost, but we didn't give the reason for being there. I think the three of us were all of the same mind: Roy had lifted our spirits and made us feel so much better, if only for a short time, and we wanted to keep the moment light and cheerful.

I can't explain how I felt, it was as though a great weight had been lifted, he had such a wonderful personality. That day, unknowingly he helped three people to continue their journey feeling so much better for having been in his company.

HELEN HARRISON

I first saw Roy when he gave an address from the pulpit of Leicester Cathedral, no less!

One year during Lent, we welcomed someone from a different profession each week to give an address at the lunchtime service, and Roy came to represent show business. He told of a man who was so sad and depressed that he had to seek help from a doctor. The doctor advised him to go and see the clown at the local circus so he could enjoy a good laugh, to which the man replied, 'I *am* the clown!'

ANTHEA HEWITT

The Derby Association had decided to raise funds to help the children and families with Spina Bifida and Hydrocephalus and as its Secretary I arranged various Charity Shows for this purpose. One such show, held at the then 'Talk of the Midlands' nightspot in Derby, was the Roy Castle Show.

It was around this time that the BBC started *Record Breakers*. My son, then aged five, watched *Record Breakers* and was a big Roy Castle fan. When I told this to Roy on the evening of his show, he asked if I would like to take Andrew, who has Spina Bifida, to his band call the next afternoon. This I did, Andrew was thrilled and when the band call was concluded Roy looked straight at Andrew and shouted 'Record Breakers!' to him. Andrew of course shouted the same back. Roy then came to Andrew, had a little chat with him, swept him up into his arms and carried him out to our car.

At the time Andrew was absolutely thrilled, but unfortunately, as he was so young (he is now twenty-eight) he cannot remember it himself. I can, however, and I have never forgotten the pleasure Roy gave to my son that afternoon and the happy way Roy carried him out, calipers, crutches and all.

DEREK HARRISON

For the twenty-five years prior to December 1993, I was Headmaster of Prees CE Primary School. As a school we often staged special shows and entertainment in the area, and through my own interests, I was lucky enough to meet Roy Castle at a Variety Show in Cheshire. Some time later I wrote to Roy and invited him to take part in a Charity Show with the children of Prees school. He agreed and it was arranged that Roy would appear at Whitchurch Civic Centre on 8 May 1980.

Naturally, the children and staff put a great deal of work into the preparations, and we also received a lot of specialist help from parents in areas such as stage-management, publicity and costumes. The format was for the children—150 of them aged between five and eleven—to present a variety revue during the first half, and for Roy to work with his musicians after the interval, ending with a special Finale involving everybody on stage.

The children played to the full house with panache and enthusiasm: 'The Hungry Caterpillar' from the five-year-olds, a lively 'Western Medley' from the older children, with small sketches and individual impressions spicing the programme. Roy appeared in the wings, encouraging children as they went on and applauding them as they came off.

During the interval the children who had taken part filled the reserved seats in front of the stage, and settled down to enjoy Roy's contribution. They laughed at his stories, sang with him and marvelled at the range of musical instruments he played—clapping to his jazz trumpet, excited by the fine drum duet he played with his group drummer, and marching 'Left right, left right, left right' to his bagpipes! Following the great ovation given to Roy by the entire audience, the curtain went up on Roy with the whole cast, as the children sang a song specially written for the occasion.

The following morning Roy met the children again at the school. On a warm, early summer morning he sat them down in rows on the grass, and then walked up and down each line recalling the show. Finally, he marched them about the playground and into school with his bagpipes! Before leaving, Roy was content to sit in the School Hall and sign 200 autographs for his young fans as they snaked around the room in a seemingly never ending line! It was a memorable occasion for many people and Roy had given his services completely free.

ANGELA JONES

Eight years ago my granddaughter, Kate, suffering from a rare skin and muscle disease, was adopted by Bridgwater Fire Brigade who were fundraising to pay for research into the disease.

Jon Martin, one of the firefighters, put Kate's name forward for the Children of Courage awards and she was taken for a trip on Concorde and, afterwards, to a reception hosted by Roy Castle. As usual there was a scramble to get his autograph. Kate, whose growth was stunted by the drugs she was taking, kept getting pushed aside. Roy saw this and went to her and gave her his autograph. In the low spirits the family were experiencing because of Kate's suffering, this action meant more to us than words can ever say.

FAITH BROWN

On one occasion, Roy and I were among the many celebrities asked by a cancer charity to create a wall plaque for posterity by casting our hand prints in cement. I was wearing false nails at the time and one came off in the cement.

'I don't know, Miss Brown!' said Roy. 'You're literally falling apart aren't you? You're worse than I am!'

That was at the height of his battle, when the publicity was so current. I turned to him and could see a little sadness in his eyes. He was laughing, but his eyes were quite sad. I know he used to put on a tremendously brave face, but every now and again you could catch that little sadness in his eye.

I felt so sorry for him because the photographers and media always wanted that very last picture, just one more photograph. He had been smiling and standing for a long time, posing and doing different things for them and for the charity, and he had done more than enough. All of a sudden I had to say 'Come on boys, I think you've enough there don't you?' I didn't want to be blunt with them, but they got the message.

But that's the sort of a man Roy was. He never thought about himself, always thought about others and that's why so many people

191

loved him. His warmth came across through television. They do say the camera never lies—and the camera loved Roy Castle, it really did.

PAT ELLIS

As a very fortunate cancer patient, who is now fully recovered, I found Roy's attitude to his condition quite amazing and a wonderful example to other sufferers.

My fond memory of Roy Castle was in 1992 when I participated in the Aerobathon at Earl's Court in London. There were many television stars there to encourage us to keep going, but when Roy Castle appeared the atmosphere was electric with admiration for this man, who managed, no doubt in pain, to do a lap of honour all round that large arena to a tremendous ovation from the huge gathering.

He gave us a wonderful uplifting feeling and instilled in us the need to show him that if *he* could achieve *his* goal we certainly could keep going the distance to achieve a mention in the *Guinness Book of Records*.

Roy Castle was an inspiration to everyone and will not be forgotten.

ROBERT PARSONS

My first real meeting with Roy and his family was in 1993. My wife Dianne and I had been invited to spend a few days with them. At the time, Roy had the all-clear in terms of his cancer. Late one afternoon, Fiona and Dianne went for a walk and I stayed and chatted to Roy. He told me stories of his music hall days, and some of the characters he had met down the years.

After a while the conversation became more serious and he said, 'To me every day is a bonus.' He began to talk about his family and his deep love for Fiona and his four children. He told me that he always used to clean the children's shoes. He said you could tell how big the family was and their ages by the number and size of the shoes. He said, 'When you begin in life there is just one pair, then if you get married there are two, and then little shoes may come and get larger and larger. But the children's shoes go again, one pair at a time, and the day comes when there are just two pairs, and then ... just one.'

I found that story very moving and later that night I wrote a poem about it. Over breakfast and after a fanfare on his trumpet, he asked me to read it. He seemed moved and it must have meant a lot to him because when I went to see him some months later at the London Palladium he read it to the audience. It's called 'A Man Looks Back'.

I always cleaned the children's shoes
The little (tiny!), patent shoes,
That covered feet fresh out of booties
Cleaned the black and made it shine,
Removing final traces of stewed prune,
And other culinary delights—known only to
   the very young.

And as they grew I cleaned a larger shoe.
Shoes that were strong enough to walk in
   (almost!).
Certainly strong enough for a toddler
To take five steps ... and fall.

And then those first school shoes
Shoes that led such little feet
Into a world full of such tomorrows.

And later shoes, the toes of which
Lost all their battles with footballs, gravel,
   and old tin cans
New shoes that looked old within a week.

I cleaned them all.

And as each night I did the task,
A million memories came flooding back,
And I remembered a man long gone

Would clean our shoes
Six children in all—my father cleaned each
     one
—As I now shine these for mine.

But children grow
And shoes are for feet that move
That take the boy into a man.
And I remember well, the evening that I
     came
With cloth and brush
As I had done so many times—
Only to discover that, of course, the shoes
     had gone.

But they will come again, those shoes
Come again to me—oh not for cleaning
     now—
Other hands have long since done that task.
No, they will bring a man to me and a
     woman
Holding the hands of tiny ones—
With little feet.

And young eyes will look up and say
'Grandpa, mummy said ... that you will
     clean my shoes.'

For Roy's next Christmas present, his children
went into the loft, dug out all the old
photographs and cut the shoes off some of
them. They arranged a collage of shoes of all

shapes and sizes around the poem and framed
it.

MURIEL PROUDMAN

In January 1993 my granddaughter Amanda was diagnosed as having leukaemia. She was twenty-three years old. As you can imagine it was a terrible shock to all the family.

During the course of the year her condition seesawed, but in August we thought things looked better as a match was found for her to have a bone marrow transplant.

At this time, Roy Castle was fighting his own battle. He was such a wonderful example of 'never giving in', I decided to write to him to see if he could cheer Amanda up by dropping her a line. In a matter of a week Roy had written a lovely letter, Amanda was delighted. We all thought how marvellous it was that in the middle of all his troubles he had found the time to write and I'm sure he wrote to hundreds of other people.

Unhappily, our precious Amanda was not to survive and died peacefully in September 1993. Nevertheless we shall never forget Roy Castle. He was a wonderful man with a big heart who brought happiness and comfort to our family at a tragic time.

Long will he be remembered by very many people.

SHIRLEY CAUT

As a family we never met Roy Castle. We always enjoyed and admired his many talents and whenever we could we would watch him on television.

In 1993 our beloved daughter Christine was diagnosed as having a rare form of ovarian cancer and we knew early on in her treatment that her chances of survival were practically nil. We were always very grateful and touched by the love and support we received from family and friends, and we like to include Roy among these. His touching appearance on *Songs of Praise* when he chose hymns that were special for him and his family, gave us hope at a particularly dark and troubled time. Roy demonstrated such courage and clear sightedness about facing his own death it was an inspiration to Christine and all who loved her.

If Roy and his family ever had misgivings about 'going public' about his cancer and treatments, his hopes and fears and finally his acceptance of losing his battle against the disease, I hope this memory of him will dispel them now. Roy gave us the courage to go on, to face whatever lay ahead and most of all he showed us that death, when it comes, can be a triumph.

ROLF HARRIS

Roy was always at pains to put people at their ease, and often used humour to do it.

I well remember a story he told at a get together of all his friends. He had been talking about his chemotherapy, and launched into this story about a crowded pub.

Everybody in the place was drinking and talking and laughing, when the door opened and all conversation stopped dead. There, revealed in the doorway was an old chap in a hospital gown. The sleeve of the gown was rolled up and a needle, taped in place in the vein, was delivering pink liquid from a plastic tube attached to a plastic sac suspended from a stainless steel hook.

The hook was at the top of a drip stand which the old man proceeded to push across the room towards the bar. The old fellow looked at death's door, with greyish complexion and sunken eyes, and everyone in the place followed his progress.

There was total silence, broken only by the squeak of the wheels and the shuffle of the old man's slippers.

When he finally staggered up to the bar, every ear in the place strained to hear him whisper, 'A large double brandy, thank you.' The barman said nothing in the hush but filled the order and stood there watching, with the rest of the place, as the old chap took huge gulps of the liquid, interspersed with snatches of conversation.

'I shouldn't be ...' gulp '... shouldn't be drinking ...' gulp, gulp '... shouldn't be drinking with this with ...' gulp '... with what I've got!' gulp, gulp.

He finished the drink and ordered another one. The barman gave it to him and everyone watched and felt really sorry for the old man. 'I shouldn't be drinking this with what I've got.' The second drink disappeared and he ordered a third. Everyone watched, fascinated, as the old man downed his third double brandy.

Eventually the barman asked him what everyone in the bar by that time was desperate to know: 'What have you got?'

'Fifteen pence!'

WENDY CRAIG

Roy's wonderful sense of humour was always evident, right through his illness. He told this hilarious story at a party he gave to celebrate his birthday and the remission of his cancer.

One day he had been receiving radiotherapy and as his treatment was drawing to a close, he thought he would play a prank on the radiotherapist. He managed somehow to get hold of a skull and took it into the treatment room. Whilst the radiotherapist wasn't looking, he slipped off the table, placed the skull where his head had been and hid behind one of the screens.

When the therapist returned she nearly jumped out of her skin—at which Roy hopped out from behind the screen roaring with laughter!

ALAN SOAR

Roy was known for his fantastic ability to get a sound out of anything which could be blown. I remember an example of this one Sunday evening, close to Christmas, at Gold Hill Baptist Church.

The service had just finished and Jim Graham, our Pastor, announced the final hymn, 'Amazing Grace How Sweet The Sound'. From the gallery, the sound of bagpipes launched into the first verse without any wailing warm-up normally associated with that instrument.

Roy had come across the bridge from the adjacent hall and stood outside in the cold until the hymn was announced, then opened the door, stepped in and started playing! He said afterwards how difficult it had been, because he couldn't do any warm-up as it would have been heard inside the church and taken away some of the joyful effect.

RONALD HARRIS

In 1993 I entered the Cardiothoracic Centre in Liverpool to have a triple by-pass heart operation. Exactly one week later Roy Castle visited the hospital and came into our ward along with Mr Donnelly. As I was in the first bed, Roy came bounding over to me and the first words he uttered were, 'Hello, Ron, you've got a hole in your sock!'

This remark immediately broke the ice and we chatted for a few minutes and of course had our photograph taken. He went to every patient in that ward and had us all laughing. He was a wonderful tonic to us all. He did this despite the fact that he himself was desperately ill. The last words he said to us before dancing out of the ward were, 'We won't let the B******* beat us.'

BILL LATHAM

I can barely remember a time when I had a full head of hair. I reckon I was born bald and started thinning from then on!

So, when Roy arrived at a dinner party at Gloria Hunniford's home towards the end of his chemotherapy treatment, I instinctively beamed at his shiny pate and pointed to mine. 'You're just like me now, Roy!'

In a flash came the smiling retort which wiped out any trace of awkwardness we might have felt about our initial greeting, 'Ah yes,' he said. 'But mine will grow back again!'

VERA DUDLEY

Words cannot express the admiration I feel for Roy Castle and how he used his illness to the glory of God. His inspiration and faith must have reached countless people and will continue to do so.

I remember seeing Roy and Fiona in *This is the Day* on BBC1 in December 1992. Roy said many things, but two sentences impressed me so much that I wrote them in my Bible. He said, 'Joy is Peace dancing. Peace is Joy resting.'

This is my special memory of a wonderful Christian.

GILL MARTIN

There was always laughter whenever I interviewed Roy Castle for the *Sunday Mirror*—even though the grim subjects were invariably cancer, pain and death. The first time I saw him and Fiona at the family home they mockingly call 'The Castle Residence' was shortly after he was first diagnosed as suffering from cancer in March 1992. Doctors had given him just months to live. And they blamed passive smoking for his disease.

I reached into my cavernous shoulder bag for a tape recorder, scrabbled around in the dark recesses and said: 'I hope you don't mind if I . . .'

I looked up to see their stricken faces. They thought that I, like all Fleet Street hacks, was a twenty-a-day addict and was about to light up. We laughed over the chocolate biscuit elevenses as a relieved Fiona fed my alternative caffeine habit.

Roy was unfailingly welcoming to journalists who would descend on his doorstep at every turn of his illness. He was remarkably open about every aspect of his life, revealing the most intimate conversations he'd had with Fiona.

In December 1993, when the cancer he'd looked like beating returned with a vengeance, he told Fiona how deeply he loved her before the pain-killing morphine could befuddle his brain.

'We have gone through the mire,' Roy told me. 'Twenty years ago there was a lot of tension in our marriage—and here we are totally in love. I have seen friends under morphine and know what strange things people say, so I wanted Fiona to know the real, real truth of my feelings after thirty fantastic years. And I made her promise she wouldn't worry if I said something stupid under the morphine, like I'd never loved her, or I'd had seventy-five birds on the side!' Gallows humour ruled Roy's roost.

When his four children had to be told the news of the cancer's return it was younger daughter Antonia who took it the hardest.

'She was in floods of tears,' Roy told me. 'She wants me to take her down the aisle. But by the time that happens my ashes could be in a little phial. When they ask who gives this woman in matrimony, they'll produce me in a bottle.'

He laughed when he recalled how he told his youngest child, Ben, 'He said a lot of his musician friends would pay good money for morphine, so if I had any left over he could make a bob or two!'

Humour is a Castle trait. Fiona, busy feeding him up with all the foods she had rigidly avoided—cream, eggs, butter, fortified milk and ice cream—turned to Roy and said, 'If it's not cancer it will be cholesterol that kills you.'

In May 1994 I followed up a tip that Roy's cancer had taken an insidious turn and attacked his brain. With dread in my heart I phoned Fiona, who said no, nothing had changed, the treatment was continuing as normal.

Five minutes later, a flustered Fiona called me back and said, 'I'm so sorry, Gill. Roy has told me off for lying to you. But it was just to protect him.'

Two hours later I was sipping their coffee and eating their biscuits as Roy gave me the one scoop I never wanted. 'I've no regrets,' he said. 'I've really had my full share of happiness, with enough success to make me an extremely lucky lad. And Fiona knows where the life insurance policies are.'

Fiona protested, 'You keep moving them!'

Laughter ruled, right to the end, when Fiona decreed Roy's funeral a tear-free zone: no flowers, no fuss, just lots of joy.

MARY DIXON

During my many years in the nursing profession, I suppose I saw my fair share of terminally ill patients, but none had that look of radiance about them, which is what I shall chiefly remember about Roy Castle. One sensed that, whatever lay ahead for him, it would be all right. Such reassurance was uplifting.

MARIE SWINDELLS

I received the enclosed letter from Roy Castle in 1994 and was amazed that someone as famous as him could have written such a beautiful letter to someone he didn't even know. As you can see, the letter is not a standard one he sent to anyone, but contains a lot of feeling and warmth.

Dear Marie,
    Just a few words of encouragement during your battle with cancer. Your good friend Mrs Page has told me of your brave fight over the years. I certainly understand what you have gone through and send my love and prayers for your faith and determination to carry on battling. I admire what I've heard about you. Lots of love, Roy Castle.

I now have cancer again and am confined to my bedroom. I have had the letter framed and it hangs on my wall, and I often read it. All my visitors and the nursing staff have read it and many shed a little tear. People can't believe that someone as famous as Roy Castle could have sent me such a beautiful letter. I am sure he helped many people in his life, but I can say for sure he helped me.

ALAN CULLEY

A few weeks before Roy died he visited Carlisle on his Tour of Hope and, against medical advice, he got out of his car to greet the waiting crowd. When he'd shaken a few hands and waved to us he turned to get back into the car and a woman called, 'We love you, Roy.' He turned around, held up his hands and said, 'And I love all of *you*!' I could see by the expression on his face that he meant every word! I left in tears.

PASTOR JIM GRAHAM

I was sharing Communion with Roy and Fiona in their home when Roy was becoming weaker. I think it was the last Communion I shared there before Roy died. I was preparing the Bread and Wine on a table at the foot of Roy's bed, when he said, 'He's here! He just came in by the door! Don't you see Him there?'

The radiant smile on Roy's face left no misunderstanding that he was aware of the risen Jesus Christ there in his bedroom. An unforgettable moment!

PETER TOYNE

At Roy's Memorial Service in the Metropolitan Cathedral, Liverpool, there were only two of us who turned up in full ceremonial 'kit'—the Vice-Chancellor of the University of Liverpool and me, Vice-Chancellor of Liverpool John Moores University—and we were duly verged into front-row seats, next to Ken Dodd.

'Ah!' said Doddy. 'What a lovely circus act you look like—just right for Roy!' To which someone sitting on the row behind was heard to add in a stage whisper, 'Yes, but three comedians sitting together's even better!'

DOREEN ATHERLEY

Castle's in the Air

Laugh, clown, laugh,
No time for tears.
Smile and rejoice,
As you did throughout the years.

Blow that golden trumpet,
Play the music loud and clear.
March through the gates of heaven,
The Saint is finally here.

For Tommy, Eric and Frankie
Are waiting in the wings.
It's time to take your curtain call,
As the angels sing.

Heaven rings with the sound of laughter
No tears of sadness there.
Take your seats for the greatest showman,
For Castle's in the air.